Remembering Avedik: The True Story of a Genocide Survivor

By Kayl Karadjian

Remembering Avedik: The True Story of a Genocide Survivor by Kayl Karadjian

Copyright © 2017 Kayl Karadjian. All rights reserved
No part of this book may be reproduced or used in any manner unless given permission by the author. For more information, visit talesofashkar.com

Cover art by Radovan Zivcovic

Map of the Armenian Genocide provided by Vahagn Avedian at Armenica.org – History of Armenia. All credit and copyright for the map goes to him and Armenica.org.

ISBN: 978-0-9989635-0-1

Map of the Armenian Genocide

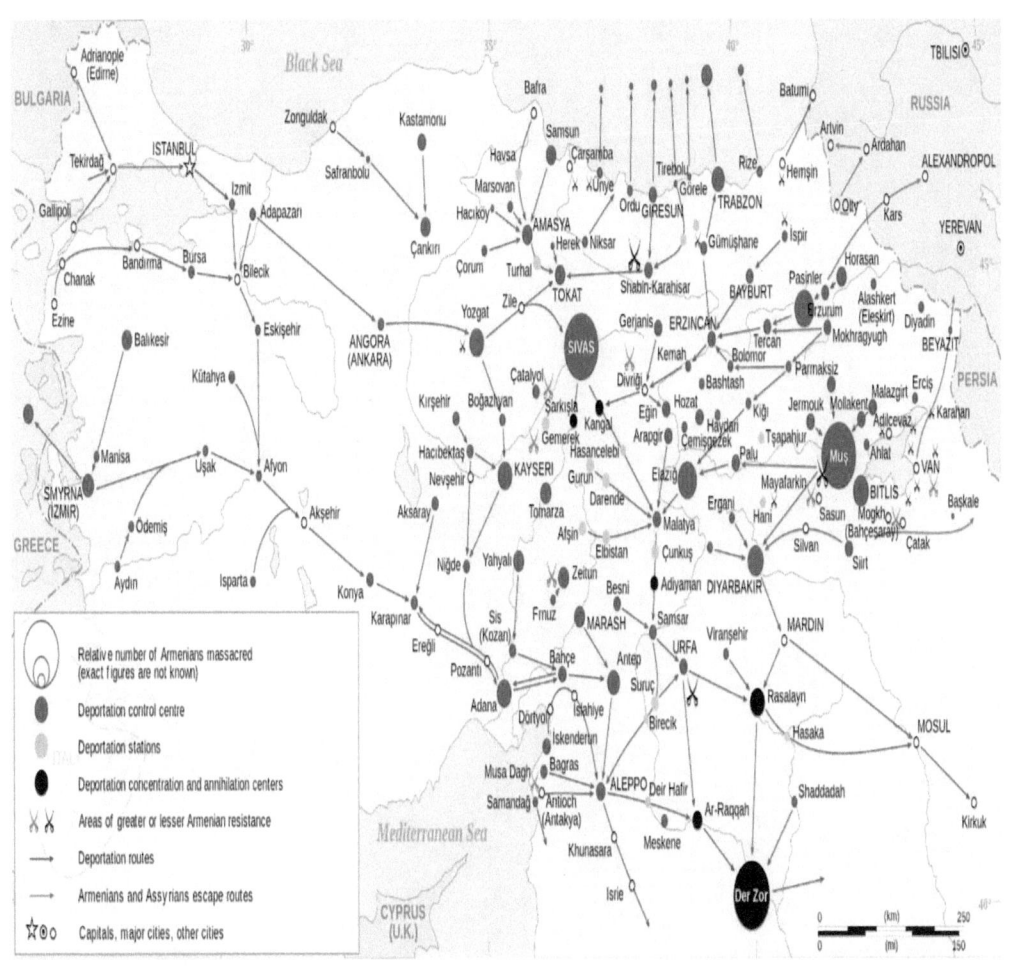

Foreword

It came as a surprise to me when my father told me that he had received from my grandmother a hand-written journal of his grandfather, Avedik Mekhdjian. By then, I was already a published writer, and when my father asked me if I wanted to publish my great grandfather's journal as a memoir, I was overjoyed.

Growing up as an Armenian and going to church, I was of course exposed to the Armenian Genocide of 1915, but it was a totally new experience observing it through someone's firsthand experience. To know that it was someone related to me made it that much more personal.

I would like to preface the memoir with a few considerations. Firstly, Avedik was not a writer in the sense that he had deep practice or education on prose, which is notable because he had an impressive way of conveying his thoughts and remembering certain details.

For example, he started the book in the early 1950s and finished it in 1958. Some of his entries are memories of when he was only a few years old.

The fact that he retained some specific names and places is evidence of one of two things: his experiences were so intense that they were seared into his mind, or he had a damn good memory. Maybe it was both.

Secondly, Avedik wrote in the Armenian alphabet, but his words are in Turkish. Both my father and my mother, who know a slew of languages, spent a good few months deciphering exactly what my great grandfather wrote. It was from then that the translated journal was passed to me, and with my father's help, I wrote this memoir.

And it is an important memoir, not just for Armenians or history buffs interested in that era, but for those who have denounced persecution of any kind. It's for those who understand the importance of family. It's for those who mustn't forget that every heart has the potential of love and hate, and that we mustn't let genocide happen to anyone.

This memoir is not meant to deride any culture. It is meant to shed light on an ugly time in history that, for some reason, has been allowed to recur in many different places and times in other forms.

Throughout all of history, just about every culture has seen some form of genocide or attempted ethnic cleansing. It is an important lesson that we as humans never forget such times, because if we allow ourselves to get carried away, we allow history to repeat.

Culture is important to sustain, as is the respect for other cultures. Humanity is meant to be united, not divided. In dire times, we must come together and stay strong. There are those who wish to snuff out all light, and we cannot allow that to happen.

You will come to understand as you read this memoir that my great grandfather was as witty as he was lucky. I would not be here if he hadn't been. There were many occasions where he was taken from his family and loved ones, and each and every time he persevered and outsmarted those who would see him and every other Armenian dead.

We must not forget the Armenian Genocide.

Table of Contents

Introduction to the Armenian Genocide................................i
When I Was Young I Was Not Scared................................1
A Gendarme's Tale..6
The Balkan War of September 25th, 1912.......................13
1915: My Second Time as a Gendarme..........................22
My Small Revenge...27
Marash's Second Deployment....................................32
Oh the Black Days are Very Hard................................35
Life in Al Tabqah..41
From Raqqa to Urfa...46
Called to Military Service in 1920...............................53
Our Stay at the Mountain and Our Capture....................61
Escaping On My Way to Adana..................................71
Life after the Genocide...81

Introduction to the Armenian Genocide

To understand the sequence of events that led to the Armenian Genocide, we must first take a look at the geo- and socio-politics at the time that were a product of Armenia's long history.

Armenia's history dates back to ancient times, with archaeological evidence dating back as far as 4000 BC. From that time until now, Armenia and the area surrounding it went through many changes. Such changes include different empires and kingdoms under a variety of rulers, geographical differences, and different cultures that developed and changed to the Armenians of today.

However, it wasn't until 600 BC that the first nation that officially was named Armenia came to be, ruled by the Achaemenid Empire. Much later, from 95 and 66 BC, Armenia came to be the most powerful of kingdoms east of Rome under the rule of Tigranes the Great.

Armenia was also the first official Christian nation around 301 AD. It was this monumental moment in Armenia's, and the world's, history that was a catalyst to the events leading to the Armenian Genocide.

In the centuries that followed, the Armenian homeland and its borders changed while under the rule of different peoples. Particularly between the 16th and 19th centuries, Armenia was under the rule of either the Ottoman Empire or Iran. In 1555, a treaty called the Peace of Amasya was agreed upon by the rulers of the Ottoman Empire, Sultan Suleiman the Magnificent, and Safavid Iran, Shah Tahmasp.

The treaty redefined the borders of Armenia and the neighboring states like Georgia. Western Armenia was given to the Ottoman Empire and Eastern Armenia to Iran. Western Armenians became Ottoman or Turkish Armenians, a key component to the events that would later come.

As a result of this new acquisition, Armenians (and also other ethnic minorities), were for the most part second-class citizens under the Pact of Umar, which was more-or-less a treaty between Muslims and Christians that listed a few basic rights to any nonbelievers (Armenians or other ethnic minorities who were not Muslim). The pact allowed Armenians the right to property and freedom of worship, but were otherwise second-class citizens. In other words, anyone who wasn't Muslim was essentially inferior. For example, one caveat of the Pact of Umar was that new places of worship were prohibited by any non-Muslim. As a result, Armenians congregated to the already existing churches.

In Armenian culture, Christianity and church are embedded in our culture for more than just religious reasons. It became our means of finding each other and keeping our community strong, something that persists to this day and more than likely was influenced by the Pact of Umar.

As a result of these events, a sizable portion of Armenians lived under the Ottoman Empire. It is important to understand that the Armenian Genocide wasn't a conventional war or invasion where one nation attacked another, but rather a massacre on the Ottoman Empire's own citizens regardless of them being second-class or not.

At the same time, it needs to be understood that the people who lived under the Ottoman Empire, whether that be Muslim Turks or Armenian Christians, all lived together. While culture and religion played a huge part in the Armenian Genocide, my great grandfather had friends who were Muslim Turks, Kurds, and Armenians. Some of these friends even helped Avedik at risk of their own lives. As such, not every Ottoman citizen sanctioned the Armenian Genocide.

There were a few key events that served as precursors to the Armenian Genocide. One of these events, of which my great grandfather chronicles, was the Zeitun Rebellion in 1895. Zeitun, now called Suylemanli, lies in central Turkey north of Gaziantep. Prior to the rebellion, in 1890, the Sultan Abdul Hamid created what was known as the Hamidiye, a group tasked with quelling the rebellions of disgruntled Armenians who were provoked by over-taxation by government officials.

The Zeitun Rebellion was bloody, but it was not as one-sided as the Armenian Genocide would eventually become. The Zeitun people lived in the mountains, and the Sultan's task force had difficulty in maneuvering their larger forces and heavy weapons through the terrain.

However, while the Zeitun Rebellion served as a minor win for Armenians, it also was a prelude into the Hamidian massacres. The Zeitun Rebellion managed to garner the attention of nations such as Great Britain and France.

As a result, these powers forced the Sultan to sign reform that would diminish the Hamidye. In the end, the Sultan ignored the reform. Outraged, several thousand Armenians assembled in Constantinople to petition the Sultan to implement the reform, only for the Sultan to order a massacre on the gathered Armenians and Armenians living in several provinces.

Historians estimate the death count to be between 100,000 and 300,000. And despite how horrific the Hamidian massacres were, the worst was still to follow.

In 1908, a coup d'état was staged against the Sultan Abdul Hamid II by officers part of the Young Turk movement who wanted to reform the Ottoman Empire to represent European standards. The Young Turk revolution was comprised of several different parties, some indifferent toward ethnic minorities while others were more accepting. The end result was the Sultan stepping down from his position, returning the Ottoman Empire to a constitutional monarchy.

Following the revolution was the Adana massacre in 1909, which was a countercoup against the Ottoman Empire in the attempt at restoring the country to the Sultan and Islamic Law. It was staged by some of the Ottoman Empire's military, leading to riots and fighting between the two groups that vied for control.

The countercoup initially was meant for the Young Turk government, but ended up targeting Armenians who supported the constitution and were thus deemed a threat. As the Ottoman military was called in to stop the riots and institute peace, they instead took part in the massacre.

Roughly 15,000 to 30,000 Armenians were killed in the Adana massacre.

The Balkan Wars of 1912, which my great grandfather writes about, were a series of wars that shaped the political undertones that fueled the Ottoman Empire's decision to carry out the Armenian Genocide. The

Balkan states at the time, Bulgaria, Serbia, Greece, and Montenegro, fought for independence from the Ottoman Empire, leading to the loss of most of the Ottoman Empire's European territory.

As a result, the Ottoman Empire retreated to Anatolia as being their last refuge on the European front. Because of the large Armenian population in the area, the Three Pashas, a triumvirate of three officials who took control of the Ottoman Empire, would later come to view the Armenians as a threat to the Turkish nationalistic movement. The Three Pashas were Mehmed Talaat Pasha, Ismail Enver Pasha, and Ahmed Djemal Pasha.

One of the more relevant consequences of the Balkan Wars was the displacement of Muslims from the Balkans resulting in the displacement of nearly a million Muslims across lands that were predominantly settled by Armenians. These Muslim refugees, poor and envious of the Armenians, would later kill and pillage the Armenians and their homes during the genocide.

Throughout the entirety of the Armenian Genocide, which began in 1915 and lasted until around 1923, about 1.5 million Armenians were either executed, worked to death, starved, or marched to death in the deserts of Syria. Other horrific events also preceded the beginning of the genocide, and persecution and violence still persisted even after it was over.

When the Ottoman Empire entered World War 1 in 1914, it was beset at multiple different fronts. On the eastern front it battled with Russia, and before the two nations went to war the Ottoman Empire attempted to persuade Armenians living closer to Russia to perform insurrections in the event that Russia invaded from the east.

Enver Pasha, one of the Three Pashas in control of the Ottoman Empire and Minister of War, tried to regain control of eastern territories lost during the Russo-Turkish War, which occurred in 1877.

At the Battle of Sarikamish, Russian forces decimated those of Enver Pasha's, forcing him to retreat back to Constantinople. One of the consequences of the loss was that Enver Pasha blamed it on Armenians, and in February of 1915, he ordered all military units to remove any Armenian serving in their armed forces in what is called

Directive 8682. From there, any Armenian soldier would be moved to the labor battalions, of which my great grandfather was sent to.

Enver Pasha's reasoning for the directive was out of fear of armed Armenians siding with Russia. Most of the drafted Armenians were either worked to death or executed outright, a key component in the Armenian Genocide to prevent Armenians from fighting back.

Following the directive, Jevdet Bey, who was governor of the city of Van, ordered the large Armenian population of the city to conscript several thousand soldiers for the war. Of course, his ploy was to execute the able-bodied men of Van to bar them from retaliating.

To buy time, the Armenians gave him five-hundred soldiers and some money. Furious, Bey accused them of inciting rebellion and threatened to kill them all. The next day, an Armenian woman was harassed, prompting the defense of two Armenian men. Ottoman soldiers killed the two men, starting the siege of Van.

The Armenians armed themselves with rifles and pistols, defending their communities from the Ottomans until they were aided by General Yudenich of Russia.

When news of the siege and Russia's involvement reached the ears of the Three Pashas, it was exactly the excuse they wanted to ramp up their atrocities against the Armenians. Just a few days after the siege of Van, on the night of April 23rd, 1915, the Ottoman Empire ordered Armenian leaders to be rounded up, and the next day, officially started the genocide with Red Sunday. Almost all of Armenia's prominent leaders were executed.

Many historians regard the official start of the Armenian Genocide as April 24th, 1915 (which is also the anniversary of the Armenian Genocide, when Armenians across the world gather to remember this troubling moment in history). The anniversary is termed the Armenian Genocide Remembrance day.

The reason for this is because it marks the first major event that occurred under the Armenian Genocide, where several hundred of Armenian leaders living in Constantinople were arrested and routed to holding centers in Ankara. This event is also known as Red Sunday, orchestrated primarily by Mehmet Talaat Pasha as a means of maintaining national security.

Red Sunday heralded the Armenian Genocide, and was the Ottoman Empire's strategy to deprive the Armenians of their leaders. Without any leadership, the Armenian communities were plunged into chaos and scattered in powerlessness.

Most of these leaders were killed, with only a few making it out with their lives.

The following month, Tehcir's Law was passed, which enabled the Ottoman government the authorization to deport anyone who it thought was a threat to national security.

Now, the Ottoman Empire was free to do what it wished with the Armenian people.

Once Tehcir's Law was passed, Mehmet Talaat Pasha ordered the deportation of Armenians. Initially, the focus of the deportation was mainly in the eastern provinces, but it spread and by the time the genocide officially concluded, most Armenians had been uprooted from their homes.

That wasn't even the worst of it.

A law called the Abandoned Properties Law was passed, giving the Ottoman Empire the right to seize any property that they deemed 'abandoned'. The homes and belongings were looted in their absence while being deported.

With the able-bodied men conscripted and either executed or sent to the labor battalions, the Ottoman Empire saw to it that the women and children were forced into death marches or concentration camps in places like Azaz and Ras al-Ayn in present-day Syria.

Most Armenians were marched to Deir ez-Zor, and from there taken to the deserts to die. Many perished either through starvation or exhaustion, and hundreds of thousands of bodies were either burned or thrown into mass graves. The case of the concentration camps was similar, with hunger and disease rampant throughout the Armenian population.

In other cases, some Armenian populaces were burned alive along with their towns. Boats were loaded with women and children and sent out into the sea to drown.

Many women and even young girls were raped, discarded like property or killed outright.

In 1918, when it was clear that the Ottoman Empire was on the verge of loss, the Three Pashas fled. In 1919, the Mudros Armistice was signed, which officially concluded the Ottoman Empire's part in the war. The Allied administration, who took charge of Constantinople, ordered the members of the CUP, the main perpetrators of the Ottoman Empire's involvement in the war, to be court-martialed.

At the conclusion of the court-martial, the Three Pashas were sentenced to death for their absence from the trials. The CUP was dismantled, although the courts-martial was dismissed in 1920 for a lack of transparency.

Some of the high ranking officials were transported to Malta so that more tangible evidence could be found to put them to trial, but they were ultimately released in exchange for twenty-two British prisoners of war who were being held in Ankara.

Most of these officials did not get the fate that they deserved. That was where the Armenians stepped in. Operation Nemesis, a campaign set forth by the Dashnaktsutyun, or Armenian Revolutionary Federation, and led by Shahan Natalie aimed to assassinate the orchestrators of the Armenian Genocide who had escaped justice.

Two of the Three Pashas were assassinated. Talaat Pasha, the primary objective of Operation Nemesis, was assassinated by Soghoman Tehlirian. Tehlirian's following trial, of which he was acquitted, became one of the more popularized cases of the 20th century.

In Natalie's memoir, he divulges the exact order that he gave to Tehlirian, saying, "You blow up the skull of the Number One nation-murderer and you don't try to flee. You stand there, your foot on the corpse and surrender to the police, who will come and handcuff you."

Still, the damage was done. An estimated 1.5 million Armenians had lost their lives in the span of only a few years. How does one go back from that? Entire Armenian families were wiped out, some having only one or two survivors among a family of a hundred.

Despite the Armenian Genocide and other horrors like it, the world keeps spinning. How does one carry on after going through such an ordeal? My great grandfather writes that he would have preferred to die instead of going through it.

I am grateful to be alive. Without my great grandfather's luck, wit, and iron will, I would not be here to tell you his story.

When I Was Young I Was Not Scared

When I was around three or four-years-old, our custom was to live six months in the city and six months in the mountains. Whoever worked in the city went in the morning and returned to the mountain by night. There was only an hour of walking distance in-between.

I remember my father making grape juice to make homemade sweets with walnuts. There was a hole with the depth of half an adult and the accumulated dirt was about the size of a man's height, in which they used to cook the grape juice in a large pot. On many occasions I would fill a bag of paper with dirt and empty it for fun.

One time, they had finished cooking and had taken the pot away. I remember falling on top of the burning wood and crying for help. My father was busy in the garden behind the house so he didn't hear me, and my mother was preparing food when she heard my cries. She thought that my father was with me, but when I would not stop crying she came over to check on me. She saw me in the pit in the middle of the fire, but instead of doing anything she just froze and started shouting out loud.

I can't believe how dumb people were at the time.

She was crying for help and when my father heard the screaming and yelling he came over and took me out of the hole. Neither my uncles nor their friends were nearby at that time. If he had not come in time I would have burned to death.

In that place there were no hospitals, doctors, or pharmacies, so they called the midwife who had been there when I was born. She made a salve out of butter and honey wax to be applied on my burns. It was only later that they told me how much and how often I cried from the pain. Everyone thought that I was going to die at any moment.

I mean, how valuable was one of four brothers for them?

2 Remembering Avedik: The True Story of a Genocide Survivor

I was not aware that they had gone to the city for a year before they came back to the mountains. Near the house where we used to live were a lot of fruit trees like apple, apricot, cherry, and plum trees. They had me lying in a bed under a black plum tree. When I had the strength, I would open my eyes and eat the falling plums that were in arms reach.

Being in that condition for almost two years made me very weak. I remember trying to stand on my feet but I could barely keep myself up.

God gave me breath and saved me from death, but we'll see when I grow up what kind of problems I'm going to have.

This was the first incident that I had. It would have been better if I had died at that time, for I wouldn't have seen the coming dark and bitter days.

This year we went again to the mountains. As I mentioned earlier, we lived six months in the city and six months in the mountains. Whoever worked in the village went to the village and whoever worked in the city went to the city.

Two months before the Zeitun Rebellion in 1895*, two men came to Elbistan* and they held a reunion with our local Armenian community leaders in the mountains. They told the leaders to call all the youth to go to the mountains at night for a party there. That day I saw them gather not too far from my house in the mountains, and at night I went there with my uncles and a few others. The two men said to party at nightfall, and when the sun went down the partiers shot 200-300 gunshots into the air. Some of the surrounding villages heard the commotion, and some Armenians got upset.

The Turks were panicking because they were always afraid of the

---

* The Zeitun Rebellion in 1895 was a response from the Armenians living in Zeitun, a region in southern Turkey, against the Ottoman Empire during the Hamidian massacres, where several hundred-thousand Armenians were killed on the orders of Sultan Abdul Hamid II.

** Elbistan, the city where my great greatfather was born, lies just northeast of Zeitun.

Zeitun people, and that night the cursed Armenians had a nice party. The Armenians felt that where the sound echoed in the mountains, and all the fields, houses, and country they stepped on, were theirs. Our youth didn't realize that their families would suffer in the future. I am writing in regards to what happened in 1915.

The majority of guns and rifles that were used that night were old. The Armenian people were not armed because they didn't have their own government or freedom. We were living like second-hand citizens among the Turks. Previously, Zeitun was governed by Turks for many years.

The government started to recruit Turk nationals from the cities and the villages for the army. Not a long time passed when the Zeitun Turk authorities began to recruit Armenians from the city and villages. We found out later that the plan was to send the 'nonbelievers'*, the Armenians, to the war where they might have been killed while the Turks killed those who stayed in town. The information was spread for a few days between the inhabitants in Elbistan, while local authorities and wealthy people came together and claimed that such a thing could not be possible in this part of the world while they were around.

After the recruited Zeitun people were sent to war, the community leaders asked the remaining Armenians to move immediately from the villages to the city, claiming that there could be an attack by night and that the Armenians would not be able to defend themselves. Upon hearing the news, people rushed to the cities and went to their homes. After a few days the local authorities asked the population to give up their guns arguing that they knew that there was a thousand of them. They said that it was better to give up the guns to avoid consequences.

Since nobody was in the mountains, when the villagers returned to make sweets from grapes, all of the grapes that had been left behind had been looted by thieves.

---

* A nonbeliever was anyone who did not practice Islam. This included ethnic minorities such as Christian Armenians.

The three-to-five year old grape trees were stolen from the backyards of homes in the villages, and a ten-year-old berry tree from our own backyard. We found out later that it had been given to the landlord of our village's house. We knew that because we had marked the tree, but we ended up letting him keep it anyway.

After, the nearby village populations who were not Armenian attacked the city to loot and rob Armenian homes. The local city's Turk population came to defeat the attackers from the villages with sticks and whatever they could find. The Armenians realized that the local Turk population of the city took in the Armenians coming from outside and were trying to help.

The local authorities told us to cover our heads as they did in order to join them and get rid of bad people so that Armenian lives and property could be saved. Such an act was done by the Elbistan Turk population.

Around this time, an illness started among the Zeitun people. They did not receive any help at all, so they were obligated to surrender to the Turks. At the time, the Turk army did not bring powerful guns and cannons because the Zeituns were up in the mountains. That's why the small and simple guns did not scare the Zeituns. The war ended, but the spoiled Turks from Marash*, Aintab**, and other places killed thousands of Armenians by axes or strangling.

Six months later after the Zeitun Rebellion was over, the Armenian gendarmes*** who survived came back home. There was a peace

---

* **Marash, or present-day Kahramanmaras, is a city south of Elbistan.**

** **Aintab, or present-day Gaziantep, is a city southeast of Marash and close to the Turkish-Syrian border.**

*** **Avedik refers to soldiers as gendarmes, which is a French word that refers to a member of the gendarmie, France's internal security unit in wartime which was originally used to describe French cavalrymen in medieval times. The reason for the usage here must stem from French influence in those times.**

agreement by the mediation of the European countries.

The Zeitun population was short of food when the war was over, so ten Armenians came to Elbistan to buy wheat and stayed at the inn.

The returning Turk gendarmes, who were someone's brother or relative, came together like street dogs and went after the ten Armenians, killing them with axes. All of this was happening without local authorities knowing. They tied their legs with ropes and pulled them through the Armenian neighborhoods. They dug a large hole in the corner of the street and dumped the ten bodies in. It was savage, and I knew these people. At the time there were no men left behind to defend the victims, which is why no Armenian came out of their house. I was only a kid. This is the second important incident that happened in my life so far. There is much more to come for the cursed Armenians.

1898 is not a year we should forget. The coming young Armenian generations and whoever has Armenian blood should not forget this.

A Gendarme's Tale

In March of 1909, freedom* was declared in Turkey and the Armenians in Turkey were very happy. We did not know that something much worse was about to come. Nobody can predict the future. After the news of freedom, the genocide of Adana occurred. The Sultan Hamid was probably who gave these orders to kill the Armenians in Adana.

Adana's Protestant Priests convention happened in 1909, where priests from every city in the nation met. All of the people in the convention had their throats slit. Other times, the priests didn't travel to participate in the meetings because the reunions were held in other cities. That year about twenty young priests went to the one in Adana. Nobody survived.**

The first result of the declaration of freedom was the Sultan Hamid stepping down from his position and later dying in prison. The new Turk government advertised a call for young Armenians to join the army. There was a high patriotic sentiment in the hearts of the idiotic Armenian youth.

The love for the homeland was so high, and the level of such stupidity was just as high, that thousands of Armenians who were recruited in the army had their throats slit and executed. Why did we join the army, including myself? I will explain in later chapters what happened in 1915.

Like I mentioned before, freedom was declared in 1909. I joined the army in 1910 when Sultan Rashid was ruling. At that time I was in

---

* The Turk Revolution in 1908 was a coup d'état against the Sultan Hamid by secular Turks. The new government was perceived to be more accepting of minorities, and many Armenians thought that their lives would change for the better.

** The Adana massacre was a consequence of a countercoup performed by Ottoman officials who wanted to return power to the Sultan. The countercoup was ultimately quelled, but not before some 30,000 Armenians were killed.

the village with my late uncle Samuel, where we owned a store selling local products. With five gold coins we became partners with the head of the village.

At that time we used to buy vegetables and grains and resell them with some profit. The local authorities used to auction groceries and whoever won the bid would go to the village to collect the goods. One day, a relative came to the village and told me to join the military for the upcoming deployment. I told him to go to my father and the people who were with him and tell them to come here.

Meanwhile, I went to my youngest uncle's house to give him the news. On my way over, a dog attacked me and bit my leg. I had to kick it to get free from it.

I realized that I was not bleeding from where the dog bit me, but his teeth had made a mark on my skin. I didn't pay much attention to it. I told my uncle Samuel to take care of the store because I was going to the military the next day. After a while, my father came back home with my other uncles. I told my father about the dog and the wound, and he told me that he was going to ask Mr. Ohanness about me going into the army the next day even though the wound was not bleeding. Mihran Magharian's father, who was a doctor, said that I shouldn't worry about the bite and to go join the army with my friends so that I wouldn't be separated from them.

Even though I joined with my friends to stay together, we had no idea that when a recruit went to the barracks they assigned each gendarme to a different group. My father came to me and told me to go and join despite my painful leg. It was morning when all my family and relatives got together to go to the city. Around seven or eight hundred people gathered in the meeting and only four of them were Armenians. There was Arsen the dog, Krikor, and the son of Boghos whose name was Ghazar. We went to the church and reunited there with other Armenians. They had brought drums and flags.

Armenians at the time thought that joining the army was going to give pride and liberty to their race. They didn't realize that this was the beginning of the problems and misery.

Being a gendarme was a pride for Armenians. We didn't have anywhere to go at night, but at least our bellies were filled.

In 1912 during the Balkan War*, if the Armenian gendarmes in the Turkish army had gotten together and agreed to leave the army with the guns, they would have given the Turkish government a lot of headaches.

If we had all stood up and resisted, or if someone had come up with such an idea, then our lives would have been very different. We missed the opportunity. If we had used this kind of idea at the time, it would have been easy to carry on; the Henchak and Dashnak, two Armenian parties that were part of the Armenian resistance during that time, were not aware that we could have taken advantage.

Anyway, we left the church in a hurry with drums and flags toward the barracks. When we were walking my mother started to cry and fell in dismay, but we left anyway.

A hundred Turk gendarmes were already at the barracks. Their commander said that all the gendarmes should get together with the newcomers and go near Zeitun to join the rest of the Turkish army. We were guided by an Armenian gendarme past Marash's market, and after Father Hosesian, the Protestant priest, prayed for us we took the road toward Zeitun with a large group of gendarmes.

In our backpacks we had food, sweets, and clothing. After walking for five hours they told us to stop to rest and eat something. I went near the water to wash my hands and rested there for a few minutes. I stood up to eat a little but I couldn't stay standing and fell to the floor. My friends who were nearby came along and asked how I was. I told them that I tried to stand up to eat something, but I couldn't and was now feeling hot all over my body.

One of them told me to take off my pants so that they could take a look at my legs. My leg had swollen to the point where it was double its size, so they grabbed me from each side and helped me walk to meet the gendarme. He saw that I couldn't walk so he gave me his horse to sit on. Four or five hours later we arrived somewhere that I didn't know

---

* The Balkan Wars resulted in the loss of most of the Ottoman Empire's European lands. Many Muslims living in those areas were forced out of their homes to resettle further east.

and we stopped for the night.

That night I couldn't sleep until morning. In the morning we left and we saw a villager coming with a carriage. The gendarme told him to take me with him, and three or four hours later the gendarme saw another villager and told me to change to that one.

"Where are you going in this condition, you idiot?" said the second villager to me as we were traveling. When we arrived in Zeitun I went to my friend's house while my friends who were with me went to the barracks. Because of my condition I couldn't eat for two days. I couldn't bear the pain in my leg. They moved my bed to the roof of the building. The wife of the owner of the house where I was staying came to me and told me to show her my leg so she could see what was wrong with it. After she looked at it she went and brought dried leaves paste and covered my leg with it.

I couldn't close my eyes because of the pain. At midnight I fell asleep and when I opened my eyes the sun had risen. When I checked my wound I saw that all my clothes and bed were stained in blood and dirt. The wound was the size of the coin and the depth of a finger. The trip had caused my leg to worsen because I was forced to walk. When the woman came and asked how I was, I told her that the bedding had got dirty. She told me not to worry about it. She changed the bedding while I changed my clothes. I went back to bed to sleep. The gendarmes of Zeitun were noisily partying while I was bearing my pain in bed.

Two or three days after that, they told us that we were going to leave. I said I couldn't go because I was not able to walk. They said that they would find me an animal so that I could come along. They found a mule and a saddle valued at two coins, so I went to the barracks of Marash on it.

In the morning a doctor came and asked us who was wounded or sick. He checked me and asked how I got the wound, and because at the time they used to send people who were bitten by a dog to a hospital in Istanbul, I didn't tell him what really happened. I told him that I stepped on something and my leg became like that. Anyway, they sent me to Marash's military hospital, but there was no doctor on duty so I didn't get cured that day. The next day a doctor came and he gave me a suppository.

I stayed for forty-five days in the hospital. The wound started to heal, and the doctor asked me if I wanted to leave the hospital. I said yes because I was already bored of lying in bed all the time. When I returned to the barracks none of my friends were there. I had sent a letter home telling my family about my recovery in the hospital. After a few days my father came and found me. He had found a guarantor so I got a pass for a few days to be with my father as long as I reported to them daily.

We stayed in Marash for a few days until my father went back to Elbistan. After he left I told my guarantor that I was going back to the dispatch. We were sent to Adana* the next day. After walking for six or seven days the twenty of us arrived, and a lieutenant came to us and ordered a gendarme to take us to the barracks. They gave us new uniforms and I became a funny looking gendarme.

I found a sergeant who was from my hometown who took command of me. There was also another gendarme from Marash. His name was Nazar and we became friends. These two people became very good friends of mine and I didn't have any difficulties with them. In forty days I became a practice sergeant. We stayed five months in Adana and we used to do four hours of exercise daily.

The lieutenant told the gendarme to choose ten Armenian gendarmes who had experience, were active, and were educated. The lieutenant said, "Take them out of the group and give them excessive training again so that when a sergeant leaves one of them can take his place." We trained for several months and my performance was close to becoming that of a sergeant. One day, we received an order that a group of thirty well trained gendarmes were going to be formed in Haifa** in order to be responsible for the gun storage over there.

The lieutenant had a list of names of Armenians and Turks who were going to Haifa, but my name was not on the list. I felt very disappointed and went to the lieutenant to beg him to send me, but he

---

* Adana is a city in Turkey west of Aintab.
** Haifa is a port city on the coast of present-day Israel.

denied it to me and said that I was going to be a gendarme soon. I kept begging him and told him that I was going to stay alone because all of my friends were going. Anyway, after eight days he gave me permission to go.

We boarded the boat and two days after we arrived to Haifa. There was only a young Arab officer there to receive us. After two days, the officer knew that there were Arabic speaking men in the group: two sergeants and seven gendarmes. They were not well trained. One of them, who had been my sergeant, thought that he knew everything as if he was a lieutenant. We used to make fun of him. When the officer would pass close to us, he would only say, "Right, then left," so we would move right and left. Any Armenian gendarme knew better than him. On a Sunday, which was the day off for Armenian gendarmes, an order came that the group that was trained was going to go to Beirut*.

They had formed two groups and separated us. I cannot explain how affected we were because of this separation. We had all become close, and in such a time separation was hard to deal with.

We boarded the boat and arrived to Beirut. They took us to the barracks and the sergeants and lieutenants there knew that we were well trained. After a few months, the battalion we were in was going to go to Yemen**, but the Armenian gendarmes were not allowed to go. We stayed in the barracks and then they sent us to another and smaller barracks near Beirut. There we met an officer, three lieutenants, and two sergeants. They were all Turks.

The officer left us there. There were like a hundred-and-fifty gendarmes and all of them were from Bursa***. I can't explain the expression on their faces when they saw us coming. We continued our training there and a few weeks later they sent us back to the prior barracks. Now, there were three battalions together.

---

* Beirut is another port city located north of Haifa in present-day Lebanon.
 ** Yemen is a country located at the southern point of the Arabian Peninsula.
 *** Bursa is a city in northwestern Turkey just south of Istanbul.

12 Remembering Avedik: The True Story of a Genocide Survivor

The war between Italy and Turkey* started. The Italians had dominated the west side of Tripoli. Then, two large Italian warships came to Beirut and from hours away from land started to fire at the military locations. All of Beirut's glasses broke. There were lots of people killed, while some others were able to escape. We went to Tripoli and two months later came back to Beirut. I specialized in the flag ceremony, but what does it help when they give you a stick to work? It so happened that two years later I had to work with sticks.

No one knows what will come in the future.

---

* **The Italo-Turkish War ended in 1912 with the Ottoman Empire losing its territories in northern Africa such as Tripoli that served as a precursor to the Balkan Wars.**

The Balkan War of September 25th, 1912

While being in Beirut we heard that the Balkanians fought against the Turks. From Beirut, Egypt, Jordan, Damascus, and Urfa*, seventy-two battalions crossed Aleppo. There was a train station named Damascus. It was the size of a public park named Sebil. It was full of tents. One after another, each one of the battalions left toward Iskenderun**. Behind the road to Iskenderun, our battalion—which had 1200 gendarmes—dug out several holes of about thirty kilos of dirt and took us around two months to finish.

Some of the locations where we dug were on the hills of Davoudie*** and Khortlak****. From this date and the coming twenty-eight years God protected me from so many dangers that we came back and built a house on the hills of Khortlak and lived there as a family.

Can you believe it? If I had told anyone at the time that after I was born in Elbistan, went to war, and came back alive that I was going to come back to this land, build a house, and raise my family here, nobody would have believed me. Nobody knows what is going to happen since the world is in constant change. There still was genocide coming up and no one knew about it.

After sixty days we arrived to Iskenderun. I had two friends from Adana whose parents and friends met us. In the future we are going to meet these people's brothers in Adana. They told us to go to the hotel to join them but without the guns, so we thought of going to our superior to leave the guns with him and come back to stay in the hotel. They went to the hotel and we went to tents. After a while, four of us were with the lieutenant and asked permission to go to Adana ahead of the battalion and that we would join them after seeing our parents.

He gave us a short answer, "We are in a war. There is no permission to leave." Then we thought, this man didn't give us a two day release so

---

* Urfa is a city east of Aintab.
** Iskendurun is a coastal city in southern Turkey.
*** Davoudie, now called Ashrafiyye, is located in Aleppo.
**** Khortlak, now called Sheikh Maqsoud, is also located in Aleppo just next to Ashrafiyye.

why are we going to go to war and die for nothing? Let's take our guns, leave, and save our lives.

We went to the battalion, but the lieutenant was not there. We got in the tents, took the guns, and went to the hotel to check in with the hidden guns. We spent the night there.

The next day the people from Adana explained to us how to reach the train station. We left the hotel and stepped into two carriages. We arrived to a four-way crossway. People there asked us, "Armenians, do you want to sell your guns to us?"

We responded that we didn't want to. Then, we got to the train station and boarded the train. That night we arrived to Adana. I slept at my friend's house that night. The parents and relatives of our friends told us to go back and give back those guns because punishment for whoever took guns from the army was too big. To be within the law is easy.

Meanwhile, two days had passed when our battalion arrived to Tarsus* by train. From there they were going to a nearby fort. On our way back we reached Tarsus where our battalion had passed two days ago. We found a utility carriage and slowly arrived to a crossroad in the night. We asked where our battalion was and they told us that they were two hours away from us. We left the carriage and went walking to meet with our battalion. By the time we got there we were completely exhausted. We went into a tent over the hill. A few gendarmes came to us and told us that we were welcome. At 2:00 am they said it was late and left, so we went to sleep.

When morning came we had soup and left. After a while, I saw my sergeant off of his horse walking because it was too cold. He saw me and told me if I would give him my gloves if he allowed me to sit on his horse. I sat on the horse and after a while we arrived to the barracks: an abandoned building with bedrooms and a small pool. We went to a coffee shop where they had a chimney and were preparing tea.

We drank so much tea that our hands would not reach for any more. After we warmed up we went to see our superior. After giving him our guns, we asked permission to rest. He approved, so now it came

---

* **Tarsus is a city west of Adana.**

time to escape. We found an Armenian carriage driver and told us that for two Osmanian lira* for each person he would take us to Tarsus.

We told him that we wanted to leave that night and he said, "Let me go and feed the horses again." He went and came back to tell us that one of the horseshoe nails was worn out and said, "I will change it tomorrow and we will leave tomorrow at night. Tonight you can sleep in the stable. It's warm in there."

We had to sleep there. In the morning they changed the horseshoe and the man told us to go and buy civilian clothes so we could change from the military uniforms. We agreed that it was a good idea.

I went and found a shop that sold civilian clothes. I realized that the owner was a hunter. I saw that my lieutenant was eating near there, and when he saw me he called me to come and eat with him. So I did. At that time Armenian gendarmes were very valuable, and he started to praise me in front of the hunter saying that I was an honorable and intelligent gendarme. My thoughts were that you can praise as much as you want but you are not going to see me tomorrow.

I asked the hunter in Armenian if he would sell any civilian clothes to me. He answered no. By that time it was ten at night. The carriage driver asked for eight Osmanian lira in order to take us and told us to walk five minutes away and wait for him. He said that he would come and pick me up, and that the rest of my friends were already there. We gave him the money, but I thought that he could take our money and just leave. I went after him and when I reached him we sat in the carriage to pick up the rest of our friends.

That night the sky was very bright and in order to not make noise he drove the carriage on the grass for an hour. During that night, we were very careful and afraid that they would come after us and find us. Even so, nobody would go out to the cold night. Not even a dog.

Four or five hours later we arrived at an inn. The carriage driver told us that we would eat and pass the night there so that the horses can rest. We asked him to continue, but whatever we did we could not change his mind. He said that the horses would not be able to continue

---

* The Osmanian lira was the currency of the Ottoman Empire from 1844 to 1923.

the journey with the weather being so cold. The world was upside down.

The Muslim owner of the inn asked us where we were coming from. We told him that we got sick of the war and were going to rest in the city for a few months. After we told him that he started to pray for us. It seemed that we gave him the right explanation and kept him happy because in the battlefield the Turkish gendarmes were screwed since they were losing ground and weakening.

It became morning and we continued our journey. We arrived at Bogazici*, and that night we slept at an inn again.

The next morning, after traveling two hours away from Bogazici, we encountered Ibrahim Pasha's Turkish officer on a horse. Ibrahim Pasha sent one battalion formed of Arab and Kurd gendarmes to reinforce the Turks.

None of them came back alive.

All of the sudden, the Turkish officer came in front of us and asked our driver who we were. The driver told him to ask us. So, my friends asked me to talk with him since I knew how to deal with superiors. I got up to move to where the driver was and asked the officer how I could help him. The officer asked me where we were coming from and I said that we were going from the military base we had left from to Adana.

He then asked me why we were going there and I told him that our battalion passed by Adana three or four days ago, and we didn't get the opportunity to see our parents and give them our respect since we were going to war and didn't know what could happen to us. Now as our battalion would have a break for fifteen days we got the permission of our lieutenant to see them. The officer asked me to show him the permission to be absent from our duty.

I told him that we had permission from our lieutenant but he hadn't given us any written one. I also told him that because our battalion was in transit he could not give us a written permission but verbally told us to go for a few days and come back. At this moment a lieutenant approached the officer and asked him what was going on. The officer said that he was asking us a few questions and that he suspected that we were deserting from the military. The lieutenant talked to me and told

---

* Bogazici is a small town in Gaziantep.

me that it would be better that I didn't do that. He said that it would be better to finish my service term and get the completed military service certificate.

I said, "Honorable lieutenant, we have been in the military for three years. If we desert now we are going to lose all that time." While the conversation was going on the officer kept insisting that we were going to escape and I repeated to him that we were not. The lieutenant then said to the officer to leave us alone and do whatever we wanted to because he felt sorry for us since whoever went to war died in vain.

After having a hard time they left us to go on our journey. We saw a house down a valley. Three or four days before we had gone through the same road but had not seen the house. When we came close to it we saw an officer with a few gendarmes and when we got closer to them, an old officer came down from the stairs with a cane in hand and gave us a signal with his cane for us to stop. The carriage driver stopped while we were still in it. The officer asked the driver who we were and like the other officer, the driver told this one to talk to us.

My friends asked me to get out and answer this officer's questions too. I went out of the carriage and saluted the officer, then asked him what was going on. He asked me where we were headed and I told him that we were going to Adana. When he asked me why I told him the same thing as I said to the previous officer, but he didn't like my answer and was not convinced.

I asked him if he wanted to send a telegram to the military base we had left from and see what they were going to tell him. He said that they had a telegram there and told us to step out of the carriage to which we answered that we would not come out, and if we did we wanted food from him to stay. It seemed that he was convinced after we asked for food and he let us to continue. There were large water tanks where animals would drink from and the driver stopped there to let the horses have some water.

We told the driver not to stay long there and that we should go before the officer got suspicious about us. So after the horses had some water we left. We arrived to Tarsus at night and went to the inn to sleep there. We incurred so many expenses and had hard times just to return our guns. The next morning we went to the market and bought civilian clothing for each one of us and changed into them. We became like undercover agents. Now nobody would ask us for identifications. We stayed at the inn for a few days. My friends went to Adana to their houses.

The hotel owner asked me if I knew how to write in Arabic. I told him that I knew a little. Then he said that I should write the names of the customers when they come and serve appetizers to the clients that were drinking Arak*, and that he would pay me for my services. After I stayed there for a month, the owner told me that whenever a customer hit on the tables I should go by them and ask them what their wish was.

I felt very uncomfortable about this. A son of a bitch came one day and gave me a pair of boots to store them for him and gave me three coins. In order to keep the boots safe I went to the store of the son of the brother of my friend whose name was Mihran Magharian. He was from my town and I gave the boots to him to keep them in his store.

One day, some gendarmes came to eat there and saw these boots on the shelf of the store. One of them held the boots in his hands and asked the owner where he had gotten these boots. Mihran answered that somebody who worked at the hotel brought them to him. Then the gendarme said to call that person to come. I went there and the gendarme asked me from who I had bought this boots from. I told him that somebody gave me three coins to store them and I had brought them here to be safe.

The gendarme said that these boots were his and that we had to go to the police station. The commissioner asked me my name. I answered Habib and that my father's name was Nicola and that I was from Adana. Then he asked me from which part of Adana and I told him that I was from the wheat fields. Then again he asked me if I was from the new wheat fields or the old wheat fields. I thought to myself that this was getting very complicated and I told him that I didn't know the new wheat fields so I should be from the old ones.

The commissioner recorded this information and told to the

---

* Arak is a type of alcoholic drink that has a strong anise flavor.

officers to go and bring the owner of the store and asked him if he knew me. Mihran said that my name was Avedik and my father's name was Mathios and that I was from Elbistan. At this moment I was so ashamed. The commissioner asked me why I lied, so I told him that I was sorry and I lied because I got upset with my father. I told the commissioner that I came here and started to work at the hotel where the owner sells Arak, but he told me to sell Arak on Sundays even though it is forbidden to. If the priest heard that I was selling Arak on Sundays, he would come and make me lose my job.

At that moment the police brought two thieves and everything became upside down. The commissioner told the gendarme to take his boots and leave, then turned to me and told me to leave too. I realized that I could no longer stay there, so I went to Adana that night and stayed at my friend's house.

Three or four days after I could see their attitude change toward me so I asked my friend's uncle why they were upset. He told me, "Son, you are a stranger here."

He continued, "You know that you have deserted the military. You come in-and-out of this house. It could grab attention and our son will get hurt. You should find another place to sleep."

I asked him if he could find me a job, and he did. I had to find somewhere else to sleep. So the head under this hat was a deserter now with a job in a small cotton factory. I worked for about a month. They used to pay me three copper coins which was only enough for my food. I left this job and found another one working on the roads. I felt really bad about it but I didn't have any other choice.

I didn't have money to stay anywhere. Being an immigrant was too hard. I was a deserter in Adana. I couldn't go back to my town and I didn't have money, so I had to do the job. One day they said they were going to build a road in a village so we left and went there. It was thirty kilometers away from Adana. We carried our beds and clothes on our backs, and went walking until we reached the end of the road. We rested for a little bit and our boss told us to gather some dirt to prepare the mud to use as adobe the next day.

We prepared the mud after we had rested. We went to a house at night and they brought food to us. It was very spicy and impossible to eat. We slept and started to work in the morning for the whole day until it became night again. One day while working, the contractor came to Adana and he tested the adobe. He said that we had not prepared the mud correctly and told us to go find another job. He fired us.

That night we carried our things and went back to Adana. We lost all of that hard day's work. We arrived home very tired and started the same job the next day. One day at night, while eating at the gardener's store, I saw four or five people from our town. I called them to eat together. They were my Armenian neighbors. They told me that my uncle and ten more people were building a bridge for the railroad. I wrote a letter to my uncle asking if there was a job or me. He answered yes and that I should go there. I went to the train station with only one coin.

I bought a ticket with the only money I had. I arrived and found my uncle. He told me to stay a few days in the tent and that he was going to talk to the engineer. After eight days the engineer said that I should go there and he would see what I could do. They were short a handyman so he put me to work as a helper. I was doing iron work. They paid me one coin per day. After, we went with half of the workers to Dortyol* to build a water tank for the train station. My uncle became ill and went to Dortyol to rest.

One morning, I was going to prepare tea and when I struck the light to make fire, the smell was so strong that it made me remember all of my family, from the oldest to the youngest. I had not seen them in three years and I thought to myself that I should go home. I went to Dortyol and saw my uncle in the inn. I told him that I was going to go home because I could not bear it anymore. He told me not to go because they were going to catch me, but I told him that I had to.

I went to the market and I bought clothing and an illegal gun. I went back to my uncle to say goodbye, then went by the engineer to take my wage for that day. I left toward Osmaniye**. I went to Marash

---

* Dortyol is a port city just north of Iskendurun.
** Osmaniye is a city north of Dortyol.

from there on a mule and found my Marashian friends who had also deserted from the military. They didn't let me go home for eight days.

After eight days I went to the market and found a carriage that was going to Elbistan. In four days I arrived there but I didn't go to the city house. I went to the house in the mountains instead. They got really happy when they saw me. Everyone was alive and healthy, and nobody was missing. A week later I went to the city to find out if there was a pending order for me, and when there wasn't, I stayed home for a year. In 1914, six months later, came the time for the Armenian exile, though I was not called to the military. One day, in a Turkish neighborhood, I fought with some guys and beat them.

At the time people gathered around and my uncles came. They knew that the issue was going to be big so my uncle Benjamin said not to go complain and instead go straight home. I didn't understand what he meant so I went to complain at the local police station. The gendarme there knew me but he didn't say anything. Another gendarme came in when I started to complain and said, "Avedik has deserted from the military."

They checked the records but my name was not there. They still imprisoned me. The next day they took me to the police station and my brother-in-law paid the bail. The commander there told me to be ready so that when my name came up he was going to call me for military service. All he was thinking of was taking me as a gendarme. I left the police station. This incident took almost twenty hours. This bad situation turned out to be something good. God gave me everything that I asked of him.

1915: My Second Time as a Gendarme

During the exile the war became more intense. Every abled person was called to fight. After four or five days the sergeant who had favored me was transferred to another location and the commander ordered the new sergeant to gather gendarmes quickly.

The commander asked who the person they had let go was. They told him of me and that I had a guarantor so that's why they had let me go. The commander said to them to call the guarantor immediately. They went to where my brother-in-law was and asked him to bring me to them. He came to pick me up and so we went there together. He said that he would come back in two days to take me directly to dispatch.

After two days they brought me clean clothes and some money to spend. My family came along with him to say goodbye. There were maybe eight or ten Armenian young men. After four days we arrived in Marash. They left us in the battalion where half of my old friends were. We wore the military uniform and they gave us guns to start our practice. After several days they received the order to take out the Armenian gendarmes.

We asked what the reason was but nobody knew why. The lieutenant came and said that whoever was not a Muslim gendarme should give their guns back. We gave them the guns and they told us to go back home, take off our uniforms, hand them to the deposit the next morning, and become civilians. We were wondering what was going to happen to us. We didn't know that a person's life was the value of a piece of candy.

We gave them the uniforms in the morning and they told us to be ready in two days because we were going to dispatch, but we didn't know where we were headed. There were like six hundred Armenians in the battalion. After two days we reunited in the barracks and they sent us to Islahiye* to join the battalion there so that we would work there and die from hunger and exhaustion.

Now the Armenian gendarme was screwed. The plan of the Henchak and Dashnak didn't work. We left the barracks and when we

---

* **Islahiye is a town east of Osmaniye.**

were passing through the market I helped five friends to escape.

They were left behind in a store as if they were going to buy something and I told them that if we had the chance we would escape. These people were not experienced. At the entrance of Marash there were people from everywhere to meet their relatives who were going to war. Nobody was there for us so we continued our journey.

After walking for six hours they put us in an inn. Forty people were in our group, with five or six being from Elbistan. We thought about escaping that night but couldn't do it. We left in the morning and saw that a hundred-and-fifty gendarmes were missing from our group. That day we arrived to an inn and slept there. The next morning we left again and arrived to Islahiye. There were only forty people left in the group of six hundred, and the guards who were with us were no longer there. From that six hundred Armenians they had divided into two groups, and now they divided the group again with only forty of us left. We were put in a tent fifteen minutes away from Islahiye and they gave us food. It started to rain very hard at night and we got wet. We realized that the rain was not going to stop so we headed into town, saw an empty house, went inside, and started a fire to dry our clothes.

That night, at around ten or eleven, I told my friends that it was a good time to escape and to go to the mountains since nobody would go out under that rain. We left to Islahiye and didn't even see a dog on the road. Walking on the less inundated road, even my shoe laces were soaked in water.

There was no dry place to walk through. The next morning the rain stopped and a beautiful sun came up. We went to the field, took our clothes out, and hung them to dry. After they dried, we put them back on and continued our journey. It became night, and the roads that we were walking on had downhill slopes. When we got close, we realized that we had come to a river.

We could not cross it because we didn't know how deep it was. We checked right and left, but there was no other solution. Then I suddenly had an idea. I told everyone to take off our clothes, hold each other's hands, and cross the water together. Nobody agreed with me. It was then that we saw a man on a horse on the other side of the river.

We asked him if he could help us cross to the other side. He asked us if we were deserters.

His voice sounded very familiar as that of one of our Marashian friends. I asked him if he was that person and he answered yes. I asked again if he could help us cross. He crossed over to us and we realized that there were four more horses coming behind him. One of our friends said he knew somebody who had a greenhouse not far from there, so he crossed the water and left. We were only six of us then. Four of us got on the horses and crossed the river. When it was my turn to get on a horse, we saw two gendarmes with their guns pointed at our friends on the other side of the river. I asked if they would allow us to leave if we gave each of them two coins. They accepted and let us go.

Word got around town of the man asking us if we were deserters. They went and said at the police station that some deserters were crossing the water. They came and grabbed us. When we saw that they were taking us to the police station we got so depressed. The next day, we heard that they had caught our friend who had crossed the water. They got him while he was sleeping at an inn. He was also frustrated.

The gendarme asked us where we were coming from. We heard that they were going to hit us. Of the six hundred Armenians, no one was left. It seemed that a deserted man had two horns on his head, which was the reason to be easily recognized. They checked us and found Osmanian bread.

The son of a bitch sergeant was a very fair guy, so he said, "Bring the soft stick and hit each one of them under their feet." He also told two gendarmes to hold each one of us from our belts and for one of the gendarmes to hit us as hard as he could. After we got about twenty hits, the gendarme would say that it was enough and to go to the next person.

It was impossible to stand up after being hit that hard, so we would get around crawling. When we were getting hit by the stick, the gendarme that was hitting us was saying that it didn't matter how long we begged God, and even if he came down to us, he would not help us because we were sinners for not believing in Islam. My turn came and they also hit me twenty times and I too crawled to one side. When my cousin's turn came, he said that he was not with us and that he had papers from a German company.

He said that he received a letter at my house to join the Army, so he went to the city to join the Army. The company's paper that he showed to the gendarme was a personal recommendation that the Dortyol engineer had given to him. The gendarme told my cousin to give him the letter. I thought to myself, "What would this animal understand from that letter?"

It was written in German. He looked at it from every angle and said that he didn't understand anything about it, so he gave it back. He told my cousin that he was going to skip the penalty but my cousin was also going to go to Islahiye. They put all seven of us in a small room the size of a bed with our hands in chains. Our hands started to swell and hurt, and our feet were already hurting. It was very hard to bear the pain. We saw an Armenian sergeant from Marash and asked him to please loosen our chains a little because we could not bear the pain. He said that the other sergeant plays backgammon at night and sleeps happy. He said that at the change of shift he can take the keys from the other gendarme and open the chains. When the time came he loosened up our chains.

We could finally breathe. At morning they gave us bread from the city. We left with two gendarmes guarding us. It had rained the night before so all the roads were covered with mud. This time they handcuffed two of us on one chain. Since we were walking on the mud we would fall and bring down with us our companion. We did not have any strength left. We walked for two or three hours like this and begged the gendarme to free us from the chains. He did and it gave us some respite. I thought that it would have been better for them to kill us with a gunshot than to make us suffer this way. We had the chance to escape but nevertheless I didn't think of it before getting trapped with the Turks.

The bad side of the Zeitun people was that some of them wanted to go to war and some of them wanted to surrender to the Turks thinking that they would not harm them. The Zeitun people suffered for it. Now we were really afraid since in Zeitun there were bandits fighting. From the six hundred Armenians no one survived and we were the last ones to get caught.

In order for them not to think that we were bandits from Zeitun, we asked the gendarmes to take out our handcuffs while entering the city. We convinced them and they let us free from our chains. It was very different to enter the city with hands chained than enter it free. We went straight to the commander. The sergeant handed him the recommendation letter. I did not have any patience left, so I peeked from the keyhole on the door and saw the commander signaling with his hand and asking to the gendarme who brought us here to take us to Beyoglu*.

The commander then left. We went to Beyoglu and the sergeant left us with another sergeant there. At night a lieutenant came and asked who we were. The sergeant said that we were brought to them as military deserters. Then he asked for someone to bring a stick to hit us. He hit us five or six times and told them to keep us separated in different tents.

The children of my children who read and hear this will know how many difficulties their grandfather went through, and the things that can happen during life's ups-and-downs like the waves.

* Beyoglu is a district in Istanbul.

My Small Revenge

After all of this happened and overcoming many dangers, the lieutenant who hit me the last time sent me to work at a military bakery. After a while, he sent me to work in food storage. It was 1917. I got my revenge on him a hundred times by making fun of him.

When I was working at the bakery I started to make a profit from exchanging goods from the storage for a value of two coins. Three people used to work in food storage. One of them, who was the lieutenant's most reliable person, was an Armenian from Aintab. His responsibility was to weigh the goods. One day, I told him, "My friend, let us take advantage of this food and make some money to spend." He answered, "No, I will not do anything illegal." I told him, "Do whatever your heart tells you to do." At the time the government used to collect food rations from the villages and send them to the food storage for the gendarmes.

One day, a hundred bags of rice came. I told Lootfi, who was a gendarme, "Let us take one of these bags." He asked, "Can we do something like that?" Then I said, "Don't worry about it. I will take care of it, and you will only take care of the guards who wait at the entrance of the storage at 5 pm and go home." He agreed.

I told Garabed, who was from Bursa living in Beyoglu, that we were going to carry a bag of rice that night. He said, "It's not the same to carry a bag of rice than to carry one kilo of rice." I said, "I will set it up you just do what I tell you to do." He agreed. We went into the food storage. Its size was about a hundred square meters. Its walls were made out of wood and were four meters high. The roof was covered in laminated metal. There was an empty space of the size of a man between the walls and roof. I gave him six empty bags and told him to fill them with the same amount of rice, and when he was done to pass them to me through the empty space under the roof. At five o'clock, the Arab guard came to take his place at the door. I went to the back of the food storage. Then Garabed came and stepped on my shoulders so he could reach the top of the wall. When he reached the other side, he stepped on a few empty cans which fell all over the place.

The sound was so much that I can't even describe it. I went back to where the Arab guard was and told him that if somebody asked about the noise, he should say that a cat entered the food storage and that you ran after it. I waited for ten minutes, then went back to the guard and asked if there was any news. He said no. I went again to the back of the food storage and signaled Garabed that I was there again. He stepped on an object to be able to reach the empty space between the wall and roof and gave me the first bag of rice. I took it a few steps away and left it on the floor. I did that six times back-and-forth. The seventh time he stepped again on my shoulders and exited the food storage. We took the bags to a grocery store in Zeitun and gave them to the owner. Then we left.

I went back to the store in the morning and asked what he did with the rice. He said he weighed it and it came out to a hundred kilo, so he gave me sixty coins. I took the money and went to see my friends to share it. The cost of the six empty bags was fifteen coins, so I was left with twelve coins. With this, I took my revenge on the lieutenant who gave me the beating. Even though it was insignificant, it was all I could do, and it was still sweet.

After a few days an Emir* came from Aleppo to send that hundred bags of rice there. We called ten or fifteen gendarmes from Beyoglu. There were a few Terter** gendarmes who came to weigh the rice. They took the bags with carriages to the train wagon. The officer who was counting the bags realized that there was one missing. Thinking they mistakenly counted the bags, they brought them all back and counted them again. There was still a missing bag.

The officer told them to call the guard who was standing at the door. The guard comes but he seemed confused. The officer then asked him, "Son, where did this bag go?" He answered, "I don't know Effendi***, I cannot understand." Then I was asked, "Avedik, where did this bag go?"

I said, "Effendi, we only go in the food storage with your permission, and there is a guard at the door." The officer, who had to indemnity and pay the twelve lira for the missing bag thought about it for two hours and asked us around fifty times. He was very preoccupied. At that time I felt sorry for him and I said that I will tell him something.

He asked me what, and I said, "Whoever sent these goods is an Armenian officer whose name is Haig and he probably sent only ninety-nine bags instead of a hundred. You probably didn't realize that when you received the merchandise. He probably kept that missing bag for himself."

The officer then said, "God bless you, you solved the dilemma. That man did something wrong." This way we saved ourselves and everybody was relaxed. He told me, "Take this rice to Aleppo and deliver it." I took the paperwork, an empty bag, and boarded the train. When we arrived in Aleppo, I handed the bags in the train station and they stamped the papers. The wagon was not locked so I opened the door, got in, and closed it behind me. I opened two rice bags and took fifteen kilos of rice and put it into the empty bag I had with me, then sewed the two rice bags shut and left at night.

I went to my old landlord and gifted him the rice. This was my way of having revenge a second time from the hit two years ago. It may seem silly or otherwise insignificant, but at that time we were so powerless that we had to take what we could get.

As I said before, even a little taste of revenge, even if it didn't matter in the big picture, was sweet.

In this life the years and the minutes change, and nobody knows how things are going to be. We realized that this job was not to endure or have patience with. Inside the tent where we used to eat under the dim light we were waiting for the opportunity to escape.

One night, the guard had not come yet so we gathered in a remote place. We used to walk at night and climb the mountain during the day. When night came we arrived at the place where they caught us. We were walking on one side of the village close to the mountains, so we had a lot of difficulty going from one side of the village to the other. It took us three-and-a-half hours. We couldn't see the water so we thought that

* Emir is a title used to refer to nobles or people of authority, meaning 'lord'.
** Terter is a city in present-day Azerbaijan.
*** Effendi is akin to Emir, used to refer to someone like 'sir'.

we had lost our path. We slept under some rocks for a few hours. It was March, and it was so cold I can't even explain it. We heard a rooster from the village. Morning was here, so we stood up and continued walking for fifty more meters. That's when we arrived at the water.

Last time, when one of our friends had crossed the water toward the greenhouse and was caught sleeping in the hotel, he was tied to a horse and dragged across the ground to Marash where he died after three days.

We were at the same village when it became morning. We saw three or four tents by the bridge near the water. We thought that they were gendarmes so we got afraid. We discovered that there had been a flood and half the bridge had fallen, so professional workers were brought in to fix it.

We were still really afraid. We crossed the bridge one-by-one. When we got close to Marash, some of us said, "The Marashian people will catch us. Let's separate." The other people in our group told us not to go to their houses. They were that nasty to us. We went to Marash. My friend went to somebody's house and I went to a friend's house in Elbistan. The first day they were good to me but the next day their faces had changed. I didn't know why.

At night, the landlord took a portion of food and left. The next morning I asked him who he took the food to, and he said that he took it to his uncle's wife who was hiding a relative. There were a lot of deserter Armenian gendarmes in Marash. The commander's announcer was shouting in the streets that whoever led them to hidden gendarmes would get a gold coin. Scared about the news, the deserters could not find anywhere to hide. I thought about going to Zeitun, but even a bird could not fly on the roads. I could not go home nor to Zeitun.

At the time I had no idea what to do. Everybody was looking for a spot for their children to hide. Just imagine the people who did not have close relatives. I stayed for five days at my friend's house, and after that I went to a person who I knew from Marash. The landlord welcomed me saying that his son Krikor was hiding at his father-in-law's house,

* Garmoudj is a small village just northwest of Urfa.
** Yarbasi is a city west of Aintab.

and if they came looking for him they would arrest me and that he couldn't interfere with that. I stayed there for six days, then found my mother's uncle's house. There they welcomed me because I was the son of their relative. Her husband had died and she was very poor being a widow with four children. One of her daughter's was engaged, and three or four days after her fiancé also came.

The house was at a side of Marash. Sometimes I would go outside to walk. The woman told me not to go out because the Turks could see me and tell the gendarmes that I was hiding so they would catch me. At that time I had to decide where to go. Holding my soul in my teeth I went from one side of Marash to the other. I found my friends and told them that I was going to surrender. They told me that they were waiting for me and were bored of the wait. The next day they would also surrender.

I went back to the house, and the next morning went back to my friends. We entered the Kalealti Church. There were like fifty confused Marash gendarmes. We went with the Armenian priest to surrender. He entered the apartment of the commander and told him that he had brought a lot of gendarmes. The commander, spewing poison out of his mouth, said, "Father, the ones who you brought are the ones who have been causing me a lot of trouble."

At that moment I realized that we were in a big problem and it was going to be very hard to get out considering we didn't even have any hidden guns. To stay in the battalion was an unbearable danger that we did not know. So what to do? The life of one thousand Armenian gendarmes was pending on a decision. We did not know how the poor Armenians could solve the issue. The poor people were drowning in the ocean without even a branch of a tree to hold onto. God help these abandoned people.

Still the Henchak and the Dashnak were sleeping.

Marash's Second Deployment

After a few days, five or six hundred Armenian gendarmes and other nationals were sent to Aintab and put into a governmental deposit. For about a month we worked on a road. After that, they sent us to Nurhak* when the Armenian refugees of Zeitun started to come. The people of Aintab gave them food, water, and shoes to help. A month after that, they brought us back to Aintab. There, I saw Shaheen, the gendarme who was Angela's father. Angela would eventually marry my son Mathios. We started to talk about what they were going to do to us and what was going to happen.

There was nowhere to escape.

Eight or ten days after, a hundred Armenians were sent to Urfa, including myself. We started to work two hours away from Urfa on a road. The refugees of the Musa Mountains came and passed by us. We went to the lieutenant and asked him to give us permission to go and see our parents because we heard that they were taking them away. He did not give it to us. Our tent was very close to the people walking on the road. We knew them and they knew us.

Our parents cried over there and we cried here in our tents. You could not resist the pain. The godless commander did not let us go. Some Armenian gendarmes escaped again and the authorities started to pursue them, catching them in their houses and bringing them back while they hit them. In order to prevent the gendarmes getting confused by the refugees and escaping, they changed the path that the refugees were passing through.

I, alongside nine other Armenian gendarmes, left toward Urfa for a special job. We arrived there and when we finished it we wondered where we should go to sleep since we were in an unfamiliar place. We decided to go to the church to sleep, but when it was time to sleep we saw two policemen come to us and ask who we were. We told them that we were gendarmes from the Amele Battalion**. They said that if we

---

* Nurhak is a town just southeast of Elbistan.
** The Amele, or Labor, Battalion was where many able-bodied Armenian men were sent to and forced into intense labor.

were gendarmes we should have been with the military, which meant that we must have been bandits from Zeitun. They took us to the barracks there and we were left with another godless gendarme.

He started to curse and hit us. He said, "Let your Jesus Christ come and save you from me."

When it became morning they sent our information to the battalion and they got a response to let us go. At the time Armenians were getting hit by the Turks, and God was watching from Heaven all the people bearing this suffering. That time God did not want to save Armenians because it seemed that we deserved to be in that situation, for we had gotten away from God's side.

When God built Sodom and Gomorrah, he had told Abraham if he found ten guns in the city he would burn the city, but the Armenians did not have any guns. What did that say?

Our battalion came to consist of a total of a thousand gendarmes. Close to Garmoudj*, there was a bridge named Kara where we were working. We used to take an hour break every four hours and we were paid a coin a day. We used to buy rice and butter from the village to make pilaf and eat. Since it was very hard to think about escaping with our stomachs empty, we wanted to be fed. One day we saw from the other side of the road a not-so-organized large crowd walking. We understood that they were deported refugees from our homeland.

Our friends from Yarbasi** city were bringing cement on the back of donkeys and passed near our house where my parents were. My parents told them, "If you see Avedik tell him to come see us." I received this news during the night and I wanted to go home anyway. Every night we used to sit and talk about what our situation was going to be. We did not know where this big problem came from. I told my friends that I was going to escape. Either I get home or I die on my way. We were thirty friends. I asked them who wanted to come with me, and they all answered yes. Among them were some so strong they could squeeze you, but they did not know how to speak Arabic and could not overcome difficulties. Still, I could not resist their plea. There was a young man named Giragos, I asked him if he would come with me and he answered yes. We took some bread and canned food along with water, and before the guard came we left the tent.

About an hour away was a mountain. We walked by the edges of it and then we reached the main road.

We passed two villages, and at the time they had given orders to the people that if they found any deserters they should let them die and not send them back to the battalion alive. We were afraid of that.

When we were close to a village, we would stay five hundred meters away so nobody would see us, and after we would come back to the main road. In this way we passed a few villages, but when we got off the road we did not know which direction we were going.

When we passed the last village, I realized that the seven stars were behind us and after a while I saw them appear in front of us. I mentioned that we lost our way, and when I was asked how I knew I said that the stars were behind us and now they are in front of us. If we wanted to return to the battalion we wouldn't make it even if we walked until morning. I said that we should go into the village, and either they kill us or we survive since we didn't have a choice. Going off the road didn't help us, so we started to get close to the village and we heard a dog barking and other noises. Because we thought it was close, we walked toward the noises. When we entered the village, we went to the house where we could hear people talking.

There were two men sleeping, an old man and a young one, and other people talking to each other. The ones that were awake saluted us and said, "Salam Alaikum*," and I saluted back saying, "Alaikum Salam." Now the ones who were sleeping had awoken.

---

* Garmoudj is a small village just northwest of Urfa.
** Yarbasi is a city west of Aintab.

Oh the Black Days Are Very Hard

After saluting them, I asked them if they could give us water to drink. They brought a large cup of water which Giragos drank, and then he brought another one which I drank. We were very thirsty. I told them that we were gendarmes. They asked what was going on and I said that we were bringing cement from Tel Abiad* on the animals toward the battalion.

We sat on the road to eat and when we stood up to continue our journey, two of the animals were missing. I asked if anyone had seen the animals and swearing on God everyone said that they didn't see anything. Acting like I was a sergeant, I started talking in a harsh rage since I was furious over the missing animals. I asked someone from the village where we were, and he said that we were two walking hours from the road to Tel Abiad, so I asked him to take us to the local sheriff. We arrived at the sheriff's office, but he was not there. I then asked the same person who showed us around that we would give him two coins if he could show us where the road to Tel Abiad was.

He said that he was going to ask his father. We went with him to his father, but he told his father that he thought we were lying. His father told him it made no difference, and whatever was going to happen to just let it be. So the young man came with us to the road and after a few minutes he told us to wait for him to get his shoes. I did not let him go back and threatened him, telling him that if he did not obey us he was going to have a big headache.

He pointed us in the right direction, and we gave him the money and said goodbye. We went into a village and nobody would interact with us. From one of the side of the village we saw a large road in front of us. We took the road, but realized that it was the wrong way because it took us to a different town. By this time it had become morning, so we were obligated to go into the town.

We went to the plaza to drink water, and I noticed somebody silently sleeping. We drank the water fast and walked through the alleys.

---

*Tel Abiad is a city northeast of Aleppo that sits on the border of Turkey and Syria.

We encountered an Arab on the road.

I asked him how to find the road to Tel Abiad, and he said that we needed to walk five more hours and on the way we had to pass five or six villages.

After we walked for an hour we saw a railroad. We had four hours left to get to Tel Abiad. We went into another village and got a cup of yogurt to drink and eat a little bit of bread. We had not eaten since the night before. We put the bread on our mouth but we couldn't even swallow it because we were so sleepy and tired. We just drank the yogurt and continued on our way. By now we changed the plan of our journey, so when someone asked us who we were we would say that we were refugees, and that we had lost our animals and were looking for them.

All of the sudden a train came, and in the back wagon were workers. The train stopped away from us and these workers got off, then the train left. We went by the workers but we could not tell if they were Armenians, Kurds, Arabs, or Turks. At the time we did not know who was who. We saluted them and moved on. After we were a little away from them, we saw a gendarme coming toward us from the middle of the road.

We came close, but he did not look at us and continued on his way. We walked for two hours and we saw the train station of Tel Abiad. We saw a miller on the road and a handful of gendarmes were sleeping there with their horses by their side, but we did not see any refugees around. We saw a person coming toward us who seemed to be a Kurd. We asked him where the refugees had gone and he said that they had left half an hour before.

Nevertheless, he was an Armenian from Urfa and his name was Kivo. I saw him ten years later, and asked him if he was the same person from the miller in Tel Abiad and he said yes. Anyway, at the moment we left. We saw some shoeless children walking by and we saw a piece of fabric left on the road. I took it and put it on my shoulder to make myself look like a refugee and confuse the authorities.

We arrived to Ain Issa*. They did not let us drink water. The bad

Arabs started to throw rocks at us and we climbed to a high point escaping from them. We saw a gendarme going to the village and into a tent. At the opportunity I went to reunite with my parents.

I sent news to my other relatives so that when they got to see me they wouldn't make a loud noise crying and yelling. I wanted to let them know that I would go and visit all of them one-by-one. We went through so many difficulties to be able to see our parents one more time. We could have skipped the dangers in the battalion, but we did not know that a whole population was on its way to die. Let God have mercy and defend us.

After two hours, we arrived at Khirbat Ar Rous* at night where there were refugees. I had told my mother to give me a black dress and black veil to put on so if I saw any gendarmes from the battalion I would appear as a woman. The Arabs attacked us all throughout the night. Five or six times we faced them with bravery and rocks and sticks. They could not take anything from us.

At the time, the local sheik's** brother came to us at night and told us he had sent two guards so we could sleep without fear through the night. I thought to myself what a good guy the sheik was. We walked for two hours the next morning and we saw about three hundred armed bandits with guns. What could the poor refugees do against them? The sheik who sent us the guards had a deal with Meloun, a sergeant, to rob us. They started to attack us. We were fifty-two families and we all grouped up. We grabbed our sticks from our tents and fought the bandits.

The bandits found the weakest point of the group and started to pull the loaded animals with goods and belongings. They also shot at our feet to scare us and prevent us from going after them. We had no more sticks to hit them with. We started to throw rocks and stones until they were all gone. We hit a handful of them on the head. They got so close to us with their swords that I told my uncle to make the animals lay on the floor so that it would be difficult for the bandits to take them. We had ten animals loaded with merchandise. We could save them all.

They took ninety-six animals from the other people in our group.

* Ain Issa is a town just south of Tel Abiad.

One of the guards told us not to fight with the bandits because they could kill us all. He wanted to scare us. For three hours I fought with sticks and rocks. I was young and strong and I did it without a drop of water in my mouth.

At the time, my father took out the box of tobacco from his pocket and started to roll a cigarette. He called to me and said, "Son, you are very tired. Let them take what they want as long as our lives aren't in danger."

I stopped fighting and sat by his side. The two guards also came by and joined us. At that moment, the sheik from the last village came with a few riders on horse. There was a group of women near us who had come from the village. The sheik made the women take their clothes off from the waist up. They then told the women not to get scared, for they were just kidding and putting up a show. They left.

A gendarme said that the people who had just left were good people because they did not hurt anyone. My uncle Benjamin said to the gendarme that they had already damaged the people and he had an audacity to claim that they were still good. My uncle said to go back to the village, so we did. We turned back and walked a bit. We saw forty people coming from the Euphrates River to Al Aqra*. One horse rider came by our side and fired his gun to call attention so that the Arabs coming behind us would come and rob us again.

Even though we had made the animals walk faster, they were tired and we could not escape. One of the animals had a half a bag of wheat on it, so I put the bag on my back and left the animal behind. After walking for another hour we got close to a village. We saw a few Arab women come to us with water and yogurt in their hands to offer to us. We gladly accepted. I thought it was strange that the husbands of these women were robbing us and they were giving us water and yogurt. We felt much better after that.

Some of us had cash hidden between the merchandise that the bandits took. Some of us lost beds, personal belongings, food and some

---

* Khirbat Ar Rous is a small village west of Ain Issa.
** Sheik refers to a ruler of a tribe.

were even left with nothing. In this precarious situation, Meloun, the gendarme, came by us and said, "Some of you come with me to look for the animals that you left behind. Maybe they are still there."

We could bring thirty animals with no merchandise on them. Everyone took their animal and I went to where our tents were to bring some food for the animals. When I got close to the sheik's tent I saw that the sergeant and the sheik were talking.

The son of a bitch sergeant was telling the sheik that the Armenians were crying about the money that they had lost with the merchandise that was stolen from them. The gendarme asked the sheik where the money was, and the sheik swore to God that there was no money in between the merchandise.

It was then that I understood that they were in accordance to rob us and share the valuables that we had. I went to where my uncle Benjamin was and I told him everything that I had heard. When the people heard this, they stood up saying that we should send this news to Tel Abiad so that they could protect us. We sent a gendarme with much difficulty and two days later we saw that a commander with ten mounted guards were coming toward us. They sent the tied, unashamed sergeant to Urfa. We heard after a while that he was hung, but I don't know if that was true.

We stayed there for ten days and the commander placed order with his authority. We found a few packages of useless merchandise. The commander used to send us some bags of flour daily so that we would not stay hungry. One day while one of the animals had gone to drink water, it fell into a hole and someone saw the tip of fabric in the hole. When he pulled the tip, he found brand new bedding and my uncle's animal that was the favorite of my cousin Artin, who later went to live in the United States. He loved the animal very much and he used to cry for it when he was very young.

After ten days, the commander took us to Raqqa. We gathered close to the Euphrates. One day we went to get to know Raqqa's center and in the middle of the distraction and in daylight we were robbed of three of our animals. After two days, we heard that our animals had been sold. My uncle and four other people went to the police station of Raqqa to complain about the robbery.

They told us that they would look for the animals, find them and give them back. We're still waiting. At the time, Raqqa's founded year was that of Adam's time. We went to Al Tabqah* and we saw about a thousand refugees. We stayed with them for a while, and many of our older members were buried there. These past miserable days and this bitter medicine is unforgettable for the Armenian population.

Let everybody know about this by word of mouth. The world suffers many changes in a hundred years. Justice Day will come. Explain this to the new generations so that they do not forget.

Life in Al Tabqah

We stayed a few days under the tent. The mayor said that whoever came from Elbistan was going to stay here. Upon that information, we rented a place in a big hotel. During the daytime everybody started to look for each other and meet each other. Some were shoemakers, others painters and some butchers. After three months we had spent all of our money and ate all of the food.

What are the hapless people going to do and where are they going to go? The language is foreign to them; they can neither speak nor understand the language of the area.

One day we heard that in Raqqa they were selling cheap watermelons. Five people with ten animals went to Raqqa with a boat. We put the watermelons that we bought inside bags when a sergeant came to us and said that we could not take the watermelons anywhere because it was forbidden, so he emptied the bags. What little money we had left was given to him so that he would let us go. With empty hands we went back into the boat to Al Tabqah.

At this point, someone from Zeitun had denounced us to the mayor as deserters. They caught us and cuffed us. Megher, Artin, and I were sent to Raqqa with our hands tied. They put us in jail. We saw two naked Armenians from Urfa who were with us when we were in the battalion. These two had escaped before a group of Armenian gendarmes were executed in the battalion. These escaped gendarmes told us of what happened in the battalion. They said that after a few weeks after I escaped, eighty gendarmes came to the battalion and the commander ordered that the Muslim gendarmes get to one side and the Armenians to the other.

A few gendarmes got out of their horses and tied the Armenians with ropes. At that moment, a professor who was also an Armenian gendarme, said, "Boys, they are going to kill us. Pray to God and run. It is better not to witness the bullets directly." Almost all of them got shot from behind. Everyone running did not know about the other; they were only trying to save their own lives. No one would escape, neither who stayed or tried to run. There was nowhere to hide.

If you went toward the village, either they robbed or killed you. For years God had saved me from different dangers. I had been twice to Aleppo, the second time in 1955. When I was in a village there, I met a Kurd who told me about the same battalion telling me that the order to kill the Armenian gendarmes had come from a commander in Urfa called Kalil Bay.

The eighty gendarmes had arrived to the Sultan village which was half an hour away from our battalion. They spent the night there and the next day they were in the battalion. A family member of the Kurd who was telling me this was with the gendarmes that night. I met the same person later in another village.

So the gendarmes lined up, and then five of them dismounted from their horses and started to straighten the ropes. An Armenian gendarme pushed one of the gendarmes, took his gun and munitions and went all the way to where the commander was and shot him. At that moment, the Armenians separated and ran in different directions, and the gendarmes started shooting after them.

The Armenian who had the gendarme's gun went with thirty other Armenians and escaped. On that day, this Armenian gendarme killed about forty men who were after them. Once night came, the gendarmes stopped chasing after the Armenians. After staying for a few days in the mountains, they came to the valley and went to a nearby village to find something to eat. The villagers, seeing that they were strangers, surrounded them. With no more bullets, the Armenian gendarme couldn't defend himself or anyone else. He smashed the gun over a rock and cursing he threw it at the villagers saying, "I had my revenge." They swarmed and killed him.

Two months after the incident, a big sickness came over the Urfa area. Whoever got sick would die in only twenty-four hours. From that village twenty people would die daily and they could not find a cure for

* The Suez Canal lies in Egypt and was one of the access points from the Mediterranean Sea into the Ottoman Empire.
** Nablus is a city north of Jerusalem.
*** Erzurum is a city on the eastern side of present-day Turkey.
**** Deir ez-Zor is located in eastern Syria, and the surrounding deserts were where many Armenians died through death marches.

it. Whether or not it was a coincidence, I do not know. The Kurd woman who was telling me all about this guaranteed that everything was true.

I met an Armenian man from Urfa in 1958 who told me that Kalil Bay, the commander who ordered the execution, was later sent to Damascus to be tried in a court for his crimes. He was found guilty and hung.

In 1914, the Central Powers entered into conflict with the Allied Powers. A year-and-a-half later, the British Empire and France came from the sea through the Suez Canal*. There, they defended against the Ottoman Empire's attack and took control of the area. From Nablus** up to Istanbul, the forces of the Ottoman Empire were pushed back.

A couple years later, from the east, the Russians advancing into Ottoman lands were drawn back due to the Bolshevik Revolution. Without the Russians on their eastern front, the Ottoman Empire strengthened with the help of Germany.

Anyway, an order came from Erzurum*** that every Armenian from seventeen to seventy-years-old had to serve in the military. The gendarme, with his teeth grinding and confused attitude, saw that all the Armenians called to serve were taken group-by-group out of the city. This happened a few times and he noticed that whoever went did not come back. Nevertheless, they were all killed over there and the remaining women and children were taken toward Deir ez-Zor****.

A woman went to get water from the spring and saw bodies of a few dead men in the water. She recognized one of them as her husband, crying and yelling like crazy as she ran toward the tents to tell everybody what she saw. That was when we realized what had happened to all the men that were taken as gendarmes.

At the news, hundreds of panicked people went to the Sinjar Mountains* and died there from hunger and thirst. After that, the gendarmes placed a fabric on the floor and asked that whoever had money or gold should place them on it. Whoever did not give anything would get checked and if they found everything their punishment would be death. The poor women brought what they had out of fear, and whoever did not have anything was stabbed in their stomachs as if they had swallowed whatever they had.

Then, they threw the bodies in a hole and burned them.

The remaining orphan children were left on an island to die there from hunger. Many girls were lost there as they were taken as slaves or to be sold. Whoever was left was taken by the gendarmes to Deir ez-Zor's desert where the people died of hunger and thirst. At the time, the governor of Deir ez-Zor went there and brought some Chechens with him saying that any Armenian life, merchandise, or money was theirs and that they could do whatever they wanted with them.

At the same time, the railroad got damaged and they heard that they needed workers to repair it. Whoever helped would get paid a bag of wheat of a hundred kilos and one coin. Whoever heard that left the Armenians alone and joined the workers to repair the railroad. They called Deir ez-Zor's governor to Istanbul to ask him what happened to the Armenians in Deir ez-Zor, and when he told them that there were still Armenians alive, they assigned a new governor so that he would finish the job.

Young Armenian boys, whose parents were dead, were taken by the Chechens as servants and told that there were no Armenian's left. They were converted to Islam by circumcision and they had them practice with weapons.

The new governor came to Deir ez-Zor chauffeured in a car. When he was passing near Ras al-Ayn**, where the Chechens were at the edge

---

* The Suez Canal lies in Egypt and was one of the access points from the Mediterranean Sea into the Ottoman Empire.

** Nablus is a city north of Jerusalem.

*** Erzurum is a city on the eastern side of present-day Turkey.

**** Deir ez-Zor is located in eastern Syria, and the surrounding deserts were where many Armenians died through death marches.

of the Kahbur River, these young Armenians were casually there on horseback when he passed. The Chechens met with the governor to welcome him, and he asked the young Armenians where they were from and how old they were.

The first one answered, "I am from Mush and I am sixteen-years-old." After saying that, he took his gun and told his friends that he was going to kill the dog. Mounting his horse, with the gun in his hands, he got close to the governor to shoot him, but saw that one of the Chechens was aiming at him. The Armenian boy shot the Chechen first, and the driver of the car froze out of fear. Taking advantage of the opportunity, the young Armenian shot twice, putting a bullet in the governor's head.

With his horse he escaped to Sinjar. They said later that the other boys escaped from the Chechens to go where the Germans were working on the railroad and were saved.

From Raqqa to Urfa

Three of us and some Arabs with our hands tied went toward Urfa. The gendarmes would hit the ones who fell behind with sticks. We arrived close to our prior battalion and passed by. When we got to Urfa they put us in separate cells. A few days later, they took us out and took us to dispatch where four hundred people between Turks, Kurds, and Arabs were gathered together.

After thirty people in front of us were registered, our turn came and the officer asked the gendarme where we were from. He said that we were Armenians from Urfa. It was three o'clock when we got out of jail and at six o'clock when the war had started on September, 29th 1915. If we had not got out of jail before the war started, we would have been killed.

We arrived to a fortification and stayed there for ten days. I saw gendarmes coming from Aleppo. What could a hundred-and-thirty Armenian gendarmes do among thousands of Turk gendarmes? After this was when we heard that the Armenian men were killed making them believe that they were joining the military. Over this news, we went to the authorities who were also from Elbistan and told them that were afraid that something could happen to us. They told us that nothing would happen to us and that they were going to send us to Aintab.

And so they did, and we arrived in Aintab alive and healthy. We were handed over to the local government office. We had no money left. One day I saw a Turkish man from Elbistan who I knew and he gave us food for fifteen days. At the time of Sultan Mehmed* when I was a gendarme he became a guarantor for me. He helped me out a lot. His father's name was Hamid and his name was Hafez. God bless him.

My late father had sent a letter so that I would give to the Armenian authorities of Aintab that they need help in Al Tabqah. I handed the letter to them but they said that they could not do anything because they were already helping the refugees in Aintab and could not help the refugees in Al Tabqah also.

---

* The Sultan Mehmed was the ruler of the Ottoman Empire or most of World War 1.

Anyway, they sent us to Islahiye and after that to the Amele Battalion in Rajo*.

There at the train station we saw Mihran Magarian, who was working as a doctor in the military hospital. He said that in a few days he could find us a job at the hospital. After four days he told us that we were going to work in the hospital as helpers. Megher and I went to work, but our other friend had left us prior to this and we did not know where he was. The hospital was at the Kurt Mountain** in the village of Rajo. They put us inside a tent and we stayed there to take care of the ill.

The help of Mihran made us feel good both mentally and physically. Our bellies were full, we had a little money to spend, and we made some friends. After five months, the Amele Battalion left taking the hospital with them. There was a military bakery nearby, so Megher and I found jobs there and used to work day-and-night. Mihran went to Aleppo to work.

My job was good. There were ten people working but no one knew each other. Every day I would put one Osmanian lira in my belt feeling very happy.

Sickness came to Al Tabqah. I received a letter that had the names of some loved ones who had passed away. After two weeks I received another letter with even more names. I could not do anything about it, and it struck me hard. I started to smoke to feel better. I stopped receiving letters, and from twenty-five family members only my brother Dikran came. I am grateful to God for that. Our destiny was to be close.

At the time of the Armenian exile, there was a gang of fifty Armenians in the mountains of Islahiye. They fought the Turk gendarmes for four years. The Turk population was very scared of them and they did not know how this gang was able to do it for so long. After the exile, when the English came to Aleppo and the Turks left, this gang came riding with weapons to Aleppo. The English gendarmes in the

Sebil Park took their guns to let them in. I witnessed it.

A Turk officer was sent by the commander in Aleppo to Islahiye to find out how the gang was able to endure for so long. The officer went to the Kurt Mountain for answers, and he reported that he was suspicious of Armenian gendarmes serving in Qatmah* and Rajo. He thought that maybe other Armenians in the surrounding areas were helping the gang.

He sent orders to the commander that whatever Armenian gendarmes were there should be sent to Aleppo to solve the issue.

The lieutenant called us and told us to go and get ready because we were going to board a train at midday to Aleppo. He said that they were just going to ask us questions and to not be afraid. He said that if we did not come back soon, he would come after us. The train came and we went to Qatmah where we slept at night. In the morning, the gendarmes of Qatmah took us and put us in a cargo wagon. We reached Aleppo at night. They put us all in one house in Bab el Djinen**. We stayed there for four days while news came that they could not blame the coming gendarmes because they did not have any proof or witness of us helping the gang.

We were then sent to Bab Eltaqa*** to dispatch. We stayed there for fifteen days and nobody asked us anything. Many had not brought their clothes with them. I had not brought anything from Rajo to wear because I thought we were going back soon. The lieutenant had told us that he was going to come and get us but he never came. It was already twenty days and we were still there. Lootfi was engaged by that time and his mother was with him. I told him that we had to find a way to escape. I told him to go to a doctor and tell him that he was sick so that they would send him to the hospital. It would be easier to escape that way. I told him that I would find another way, too.

One day, a sergeant from dispatch took around ten gendarmes to bring water from the bath. They went with buckets, and I grabbed some buckets to follow them. When I reached the door, the gendarme saw

---

* Rajo is a city in northwestern Syria near the border of Syria and Turkey.
** The Kurt Mountain lies further northwest of Rajo.

me and asked me where I was going. I told him that I was going to bring water to wash my face. He let me go.

The sun had yet to come up. We entered the bath and saw a long passage in front of us. The ones in front of me continued, but I stopped. The sergeant asked me why, and I told him that I was going to pee and I would catch up with them when I was done. He continued with the others. I went out from the bath and saw a guard to my right. I went left and went straight until I got out of dispatch. I went right into the Bab el Nasser market and passed through shoe stores and fruit stands on my way to my previous landlord's house.

I had left an Austrian military uniform with him for some money. That same day I saw Megher, who was working as a servant at an officer's house. I took a bottle of whiskey from him and left. I went to Lootfi's house and went to the train station along with his mother. That day they left with the train. The sergeant of the train station saw me and asked who I was. I said that I was a gendarme. Then he asked me what I had in my bag, and I told him about the whiskey. He took the bottle and drank a shot.

He asked my name and I told him that I was Megherditch, the son of Antranik. He let me go. At the time, gendarmes and civilians were forbidden to drink. The penalty was prison. When I arrived to Bab Al Faraj*, I saw my Armenian friend who was working with the doctor and had helped Lootfi. He told me that the dispatch officer was looking for me. They even found the gendarme at the train station and gave him a penalty for letting me go, saying that I bribed him.

After eight days I went to Rajo on the train. The lieutenant there called me and asked me what had happened in Aleppo and what kind of questions they had asked me. I told him that they had given me a job as an assistant for one of the officers. He asked me for written proof, and I told him I didn't have it. He told me to come back the next day so that he could give me my prior job back.

* Qatmah is a village east of Rajo.
** Bab el Djinen is a section in Aleppo.
*** Bab Eltaqa is a village southwest of Aleppo.

I went to the village and stayed sick in bed for forty days. At the time in Nablus, the Turks were losing the battle. Every day, five or six battalions would pass through train or walk through Rajo, and it was tense. I gathered my belongings and went to Aleppo by train. After three days, the English came to Aleppo. The world stood up in happiness. The ones who survived the exile started to feel confident that they would be safe, but we did not know that there was still a lot of danger coming toward the Armenians. The English came to Aleppo in the last months of 1918. It had been two months since the English were in Aleppo when they did the Armenians a 'favor'.

They spread the word between the Arabs of Aleppo that the Armenians were a harmful race and the Arabs ended up killing about six hundred Armenians because of it. The people got confused about how this could happen while the English were present. Someone went to the commander for help. They were having tea.

The massacre lasted for two-and-a-half hours. When the English gendarmes came the Arabs left. After, we heard a rumor that all of this happened because the English did not give the Arabs their independence. The English held thirty Arabs responsible and punished them by killing them on electric chairs.

In a shameful way, the English said that whoever had lost a family member in the massacre should come to them to get a hundred English lira for each person who died. Every Armenian near Aleppo came for help from the English to go back home because the majority of them had miserable lives. The English started to send carriages full of Armenians back to their home villages. At this time, the English were in Marash and Aintab.

I wanted to go home, but I was waiting for my brother Dikran to come with me. After waiting for a few months I left without him. I arrived to Marash and stayed there for ten days and thought of going to Elbistan to see what was happening there. I went with five people to Elbistan and after a week we became twenty people. After they had thrown out all the Armenians, they had looted everything there. The Sultan ordered whoever came back could get back their belongings.

I stayed for two months in Elbistan, then went to Marash again and saw Dikran there. I stayed for a few weeks in Marash before going back to Elbistan with four or five families. I left Dikran in Marash so that he could learn to ride a horse.

The English left Marash and the French came. The Sultan gathered his forces one more time and started to persecute and kill the Armenians. We escaped in the rain but encountered hail. Zeitun got dominated again and surrendered to them. Whoever had survived the genocide before were killed or taken away again. Saimbeyli* stayed a year-and-a-half surrounded by the Turks. There were no animals left, and no food or water. They finally gave up and only one out of every hundred survived. At the time that Saimbeyli was bleeding, the dirty son of a bitch French forces sat in Adana only a hundred kilometers away doing nothing to save the poor people of Saimbeyli.

The Turkish forces came close to Marash with the intention of attacking, but did not come into the city because the French were there. The Marashian Turks trusted neither the French nor the Armenians. They left suddenly, leaving behind their houses and going into the nearby villages. Twenty four hours after the Turks left Marash, a telegram came to Elbistan saying that Turk refugees were coming from Marash and that they should be accommodated.

Three days passed waiting for the Turks to come but no one showed up. At the time, the Armenians of Marash were looting the homes of the Turks who had left. The French left Marash by night and when the Turks heard this they came back and hung the Armenians. This was the gift from the French to the Armenians. At this news I was very worried about my brother Dikran because I did not hear from him. I later learned that he was alive.

At night, when I was getting ready to sleep, I heard the patio doorbell and asked who it was. The man said he was a sergeant and that I should open the door. I opened the door and saw him and ten more gendarmes with him. I asked them what had happened and they said that my presence was needed at the police station. I told them that I had

* The Kizilirmak is a river east of Ankara.
** Cilicia is an ancient name for the region that comprises Turkey's southern regions close to Cyprus.

to go inside to wear my clothes and shoes. He asked who was on the second floor and I told him that it was my neighbor, Melkon.

The sergeant told me to get him because he was coming too. We started to wonder what they were going to do to us. We were still at the police station when morning came. After we left during the night,

---

Melkon's wife had gone to the sheriff's house and told him everything that had happened to us.

We were taken to the police station because the previous night some Turks from Marash came to visit the house of a wealthy Turk in Elbistan, and they said that there were some Armenian gang members hiding in Elbistan. The lieutenant on duty had sent the sergeant to look for us and take us to the police station without the sheriffs knowing. When Melkon's wife told them what happened, they told her to go back home and that they would let us go in the morning.

The doorbell at the police station rang, and the police opened the door and saw the relative of the sheriff who liked Armenians.

He came in saying good morning to us and telling us that we shouldn't be afraid because he was going to get us out. He left, and after a little while an order came to free us. Everyone went back to their homes.

Winter came and one more time somebody knocked on the door by night. I asked who it was and the man said that he was my neighbor. I opened the door and saw the sheriff and a lieutenant. They told me not to be scared but to go to my bed and cover up because they were going to check my house. They checked everything, even under the bed. They left without finding anything. That night, every Armenian's house was checked.

We later learned what they were after. One night, an Armenian coming to the village had wrapped his head because it was too cold. A local Turk, seeing the man, thought that he was a gang member from Zeitun. He went to the police station and reported it, so they ended up checking all the Armenian homes that night.

This was one of the only incidents between the Elbistan Turks and Armenians. In 1893, the war of Zeitun was over and in 1894 ten Armenians came to Elbistan to buy wheat. Bandit Turks killed these Armenians. That same night, my aunt who owned an inn had a beautiful, large wood door that nobody else in the village had, and by jealousy they came at night and burned the door down. We were there in that moment. My father and uncles, with water and adobe, were able to extinguish the fire and saved the entire house from burning.

The sheriffs did not know about this. This was the second thing that the bandit Turks did against Armenians in Elbistan.

Called To Military Service in 1920

Arsen and Melkon had paid sixty Osmanian lira to get free of military service. Mustafa Kemal* got strong after the Battle of Marash** and started war in Aintab, and Misak and I were called for service. Two-hundred-and-eight officers put us at dispatch near the city. At the time the French were in Adana, so the Turks would not dare fight. They took us to Adana's surrounding mountains where there was a small city with a train station.

We did not have a chance to escape on the road. We got to Konya*** and they left us at dispatch. It had been thirteen days since I left home. That night I had a dream that we had a chicken, and the chicken's chick came and stood on my shoulder. I told this to Misak in the morning, telling him that we had a child as a joke. We stayed fifteen days in Konya, and then they sent us walking to Ankara****. In the places where we were passing, the Greeks and Turks had battled two months prior and the Turks had burned the Greeks' homes and killed their animals.

After about ten days we got to Ankara. We stayed there for fifteen days and ate raw boiled wheat. If you can eat it, you will. One day, we saw that Giragos was also a gendarme in our regiment. He told us that he had a son two weeks ago. About twenty or thirty of us grouped and held a party for him.

They put us in a train and took us to Keskin*****. The gendarme there started to write down everybody's profession and their intention was to send us to the Amele Battalion. Our only thoughts at that time were how to escape the military. All three of us told him that we were fisherman thinking they were not going to need us.

---

* Mustafa Kemal was a military commander during World War 1 and would later became Turkey's first president.
** The Battle of Marash of 1920 was a battle between the French occupying Marash and the forces of Mustafa Kemal.
*** Konya is a city south of Ankara.
**** Ankara is a large city that lies in the center of Turkey.
***** Keskin is a town east of Ankara.

The gendarme ended up telling the commander that there were three fisherman, and the commander tasked us with fishing in the Kizilirmak*, or Red River. The gendarme came back and told us the news, and we responded that we were not professional fishers and that we used to fish in the small rivers with nets. We couldn't possibly fish in the Red River, and that was our ticket. They took us to Amele Battalion and gave us picks and sticks to work.

At the time of the Sultan, there were twenty-two Armenian battalions, and because of being Armenian you had to work hard and have a miserable life while you were at it.

The Sultan's plan was to either work the Armenians to death or have them die in battle as he gathered the Armenians as gendarmes. The English and the French were the ones who started this all, going in-and-out of Cilicia**. "Let God dry them until their roots, amen," was what the Sultan must have thought. There was no other way to describe the thought behind his actions.

Anyway, it was about time to escape. Giragos used to sleep in a house, and Misak and I in another house. We were gathering bread and hid it for the trip. Giragos did not have money, so we were also giving him some bread to hide. We were planning to walk for ten days without stopping at any village to eat. One day, we told another person from Marash to come with us and he said that he would reunite with Giragos. They had to leave before we did, and Misak and I would join them after.

The night of our escape everything was going as planned. The sergeant was playing cards with an officer outside and around five gendarmes were serving them. We got ready inside, and Misak went out and told the guard that he needed to use the bathroom. After five minutes, I went out with my bag on my back. The bag was big and full, and when the gendarme saw me he said, "Avedik is escaping."

I jumped six steps of stairs at once. It was dark outside. I ran for five minutes and then stopped. Ten people started to look for me. They

---

* The Kizilirmak is a river east of Ankara.
** Cilicia is an ancient name for the region that comprises Turkey's southern regions close to Cyprus, where a majority of Armenians lived and preserved their culture.

looked for us with a light at night at the border of the village. "This side or the other side," they would say. After taking some time to catch my breath, I started to look for Misak. Coughing and whistling, I was able to find him. We sat there for a half hour waiting for Giragos and the Marashian to join us. They did not show up.

We continued until we found the road that we had to take. We walked for two hours and then stopped, thinking maybe Giragos would come. No one came. At the time, the escaping of an Armenian was not easy because if they caught him it was a death sentence. The Sultan knew how to use other people's softness and the weakness of the world. Armenians did not have any value.

We walked for another five hours and we saw another deserter. Misak wanted to rob him. I said, "What a great idea. We rob this poor man, and we still have ten days to walk. Maybe we can get robbed or killed too." He shut up quick, and we continued on our journey.

We were close to the mountain in the morning, and we were about to pass a small cave when it started to snow. We decided to go inside the cave and sit inside for a while. Hours passed like this. One of us would sleep while the other stayed awake. A Kurd close to us came and stayed for a little bit then left.

When it became night we chewed a bit of bread and left. It was still snowing and we could not see the dirt anymore. We were going to turn left but we could not see the road. We were forced to walk between the mountains. Not even the Devil would come out at this time. God, how hard of a night it was. Whoever saw our situation would prefer to be a gendarme for ten years instead of going through all this, but what could we do? It's just what we had to face.

We climbed the mountain for two hours and reached a plateau. It was snowing so hard that the height reached our teeth. We were on the edge of death. Misak was in front of me. It was so cold, we did not want to even open our mouths. We gave up talking. After a while I was going to tell Misak something, but my jaw would not open.

I touched Misak's back and found that he was in the same predicament. I gestured to my backpack so that he would take a piece of bread. We continued for another three hours on the top of the mountain, then started going downhill for a further two hours. It was morning by this time. We were close to a city. We saw a police station in front of us and passed it.

We walked for about an hour and at the end we found a house with a tall wall in front of us. We sat beside the wall. We stayed there for ten minutes and Misak started to snore, so I woke him up and told him we had to continue our journey. We entered the city and had walked for a little bit until we saw a gendarme on horseback coming toward us.

We dove into a corridor and found that it was a dead end. The gendarme passed us. We came out of our hiding spot and started to walk again. We saw a young boy and we approached him. He looked Armenian.

We asked him what his name was and he gave me an Armenian one. We asked him where he was going and he said that he was going to the bakery. We asked him to take us to an Armenian church but he said that he could not come with us because it was late, but he would explain how to get there.

We found the church and saw that there were about thirty Armenian refugees there. We saw one of our friends from Marash who had escaped a few days before from the hospital and came here to hide. He had a lot of courage to come to the city. We gave him money to buy bread, sugar, tea, and charcoal.

He came back and we ate, got warm and slept. God saved us from the storm. I had no money left and Misak had only two Osmanian liras left. I asked him to break the money and he gave me the coin while hiding the other one. If we had broken the coin in the city we would have gotten twelve-and-a-half coins, but because we did it where we were they gave us only twelve. Did this man think that he was going to live forever?

We decided to use that money to pay for our liberty if we got caught. Misak told me to go and ask for some money from the priest, so I went. There were two priests there, and I told them my story. One of them advised me to stay and not leave because we could get killed. The other said that since we were from the area near Zeitun not to be afraid because we were brave.

He told the other priest to give us the money, but the first priest said that he did not have any. A small boy who was there told us to ask the church's secretary. We went and he told us that he had only three coins. I took it, and we bought some more bread. The same boy took us to the main road.

We walked all night and hid during the day, telling ourselves that tomorrow would be another day and that God was with us. At night we left again and walked for three or four hours, and when we saw a dog crossing our path we realized that we were close to a village. We tried to go further away from the road, and the dog started circling us. We were afraid that he might bark, so we started running. We were followed by more dogs.

We ran for almost twenty minutes. Our clothing was drenched in sweat. We came close to a valley and hid behind some rocks. The dogs came close, but because they didn't see us they went back. We sat for half-an-hour to catch our breath. Nevertheless, the dogs would not come close to bad people. We went back to the road and everything was frozen. It was February.

We got close to a city but could not find anywhere to sleep. We decided to climb the mountain so we could rest. When we arrived to the top we saw twenty villages in front of us. We found a small place and stayed there over the night. It came morning, and Misak was still sleeping. I saw two people with mules behind them coming toward us, with another person behind them. When they got close I woke Misak up, telling him that people were coming.

They came by us and saluted us with saying, "Salam alaikum." They sat in front of us and asked us where were coming from and where we were going. We said that we came from there and we were going somewhere else. They asked us why we were in an open area because a villager could see us and tell the authorities to get us. I told them that we could not find a better place.

I asked them what the names of the villages were. He started to give the names and said that there was an Armenian village with ten families left. I told myself that when these men left, I would go to that village and get a hot plate of food and rest. When they left I told Misak to come with me, but he wanted to follow the path instead.

I started to walk toward the village and he came after me. At the border of the village we saw a woman washing clothes in the water. She looked Armenian, so I got close to her and spoke to her in Armenian. When the woman knew that we were Armenian, she said in Turkish that there was a sergeant in the village and that we should not go in because they would detain us. We saw four people approach us. We wanted to go to the road but they told us, "Come here. Where are you going?"

We were forced into the village. We were in a corridor when a door opened and a sergeant came out. He said, "Looks like there was nowhere to go. You came directly to me." I said that the road had taken us here.

Did they identify us because of two horns on top of our heads?

He put us in a stable and after a while somebody came and told us that if we gave the sergeant some money, he would let us go. We said that we did not have any money. I told him that I had only what was in my wallet and gave it to him. He took it, but came back and said that the sergeant did not accept. Again, we told him that we did not have any more money, and after going and coming back three times, the sergeant finally accepted. He told us to follow him and that the gendarmes were gone.

We went into a room and saw a sheriff. The reason for the sergeant to let us go was not the money, but because the locals had asked the sheriff to help us. We went to a house where they welcomed us with a table served with food and I told them that I had two things to tell them. They said, "Let's eat first and then we talk." After we ate, they said, "Let's talk."

There were about ten people. I asked every one of them their names. Artin, Toros, Garabed, and on and on. Then I told them that all of them were Armenians, and so were we. After going through a lot of dangers we came here because of you, and you put us in the mouth of the wolves. The sheriff apologized to us and blamed the locals' attitudes to us. He gave me the three coins back.

I asked them to take us to a safe house so we can rest and get warm. They took us to one and we slept there. We left at night. After two hours of walking we lost our path. Misak knew about the stars and I would remember the roads we passed. We went back and found our path again. We stayed on the path for a little bit until the next morning.

We saw a village in front of us and we went to one side of the road. There was a mill on a small river and we passed by it. The water was frozen and the miller was not working. We walked for another hour and saw a cave where we stayed until night. At night we continued walking. We reached a small hill with a village behind it. We went around it to the right.

We walked for another few hours until we arrived at a river. We did not have the courage to go in the mud to continue. I said that on running water there should be a bridge somewhere.

We walked for two hours at the edge of the water until we saw a bridge. When we passed through it, it was already midnight. When we looked up we saw two people coming, but we did not have time to hide so we stopped right there and asked them who they were.

They answered that they were travelers and asked us the same question. We said that we were also travelers. When we got close, we saw that they had guns hanging from their shoulders and told us that they were deserters. We said that we were deserters, too. They were standing on one side of the road and we were on the other. We exchanged some information about the roads that we came from. They had been close to Kizilirmak and passed by. They told us that close to the bridge was a village and that gendarmes were there.

We separated. Misak and I took off our shoes to drink water from the river. As we went down the riverbank we thanked God that we did not slip because falling into the water at night would have been yet another dangerous situation. We walked until morning, then found a cave and went to sleep. Our shoes were worn out so we repaired them with a piece of leather that I had.

We left at night and we passed Kayseri*, continuing when we saw four roads in front of us with no idea which one to take. We took one

---

* Kayseri is a city in central Turkey that lies north of Adana.

at random and continued. We walked for two hours and saw a police station. We turned right from there and like trained dogs we passed the barracks. We walked in the fields for several hours before we heard travelers' voices nearby, which meant that we were close to the main road. We slept in the fields.

After walking for a few days we encountered other travelers and walked together for a while until they took another path and told us which road to take to Elbistan. We joined other travelers who were Kurds from Kayseri and who liked Armenians. We arrived to a village, but they did not go to an inn and told us to follow them to somewhere they knew that was dry land.

Our Stay at the Mountain and Our Capture

There was a lot of wood, so we burned it to get warm. We followed the Kurds since they were familiar of the area. The road and trees were full of snow. Anyway, we reached an open space and we gathered enough wood there to burn it. We waited so that the flame weakened until we could come close to the fire and sit by it. Our faces got red from the heat, but our backs were frozen from the cold. We turned around and then our backs would burn while our faces froze. We sat like this for several hours.

They told us not to go to the village alone because we were strangers and could get captured. We asked them to come with us because they were known at the village, but they did not want to do it. We separated from them and continued in the snow with difficulty. After walking for a few hours, we found a small river and crossed it. There was a high rock and we sat on it. I came down from the rock and started to walk when I noticed a gendarme on horseback behind a hill.

We had been found.

I stopped where I was, and Misak came by me. The gendarme asked us who we were and we answered that we were travelers. Then he asked what we were doing here, and we told him that we had lost an animal and were searching for it. He then asked us where we were from and we said Elbistan. He said that we weren't on the road to Elbistan and that we were deserters. We begged the gendarme to be kind toward us and let us go.

We understood that he wanted money from us. I didn't have any money, and Misak only had one Osmanian lira but had decided not to break it into coins when he had the chance. I had told him many times to break it into coins, but he hadn't accepted and we needed that money now. Misak started to walk after the gendarme, begging. The gendarme didn't bother to look back. I wanted to give Misak the signal to take the gun so that we could tie the gendarme with ropes, but how could I explain it to Misak?

If I said it in Armenian, the gendarme would know who we were. If I said it in Turkish, he would understand what I was saying.

I was forced to offer him my watch that was worth twelve coins and hope for the best. The gendarme looked at it and he said that it looked like a watch worth two coins. It was not enough to let two people go, so he gave it back to me. I swore that I did not have any money. He believed me, and asked for the watch again. After he took it, he told us to go back from the road that we had just come from and cross the mountain to the other side where we would find the road. He then left.

We climbed the mountain toward the path. The snow was soft and covered us to our belts. We kept stepping on holes and we had to depend on the other to help us out. We started downhill, and when we got to the bottom we saw the road. The next village was familiar to me and I knew someone from there. I found his house. He had two wives because he had taken the second without consent. The two of them knew me, and spread a rug by the fire for us.

I asked them where Hussein was and they responded that he was in the mountain looking for wood. After a while he came, and we saluted each other. Somebody came in behind him, saw us, and realized that we were deserters. He took Hussein out to talk to him in private. They spoke, came back, and then went out again. The youngest woman came by us and said, "Your soul be alive, Avedik. These two shameless men are going to kill you tomorrow. My husband is going to take you to the road and the other man is going to shoot you."

I thanked her very much. After the exile, there was only one Armenian house left in Gurun*. We went there right away. We greeted them in Armenian. They had not seen any Armenians for many years. Their welcome was very warm because they were so happy. We sat with them, a woman and her young son, who was much respected in the town. I told him what Hussein's wife had told me, and the mother told him to go and bring that dog to them. The young man went and came back with Hussein, and the young man said to Hussein, "Tomorrow you are going to take them to the edge of the village and show them the road. Avedik is going to give you hand written paper that you will bring back to me." Hussein agreed and left.

---

* Gurun is a town east of Kayseri.

Then, they prepared hot food for us and made us beds, insisting that we stay a few more days. In the morning, they had prepared hot bread for us to take. We left with Hussein.

The fields were full of snow and we were walking in the middle of the road. After walking for a while, we approached familiar fields. Many of the people there recognized us and would say, "Avedik and Misak are back." There, we went to a friend's house whose grandfather was about ninety-years-old. He was very happy to see us alive and gave us his blessings. We only had six hours left to reach the city, and once more we left at night.

We arrived to Elbistan and first went to Misak's house. He practically jumped off my shoulders into his house. I went to my own home at ten o'clock and my wife was breastfeeding our son Mathios. We went through so many headaches because of the Turks. We had been away for three-and-a-half months. After all that, we got caught again because of Melkon.

One night, Melkon and I were having food at his house. Melkon's grace period ran out, so he was called again to serve in the military. The neighbors told us that a sergeant and the sheriff were looking for us. We left immediately from the patio's small door into other houses. Melkon went into one house, and I in another. I found Megher in the one I went into, and the two of us went into the straw house by the stable.

The sergeant went into Melkon's house and found that nobody was there despite there being two plates in one of the rooms. He told the sheriff that two people had escaped and they started to look everywhere for us. After finding the patio door, they started to look for us in other houses. They came to the house that we were in. The sergeant and sheriff came in while some gendarmes stayed outside. We did not have anywhere to go. Megher went into the straw and asked me to cover for him. I gave him two short sticks with holes so he could breathe. I wanted to hide in a spot by the oven, but couldn't fit. I went into the stable and stood up by the horse praying that the gendarmes did not know who I was and the sheriff thinking that I was a guest.

They came and passed by me as they went into the straw house but did not find anybody.

The sheriff came to me and asked me if I was the son of Mekhdje. I told him that I was not and that I had come from Yarpuz* as a visitor. He handed me to a gendarme. The Armenian neighbors offered the sheriff twelve coins so that he would set me free but he did not accept. They took me and left me at the barracks. I testified that I had not escaped from the military. I had a permit from Kastamonu** and I was from the Twenty-Second Labor Battalion but I was robbed on my way. The officer said that if I was telling the truth, I should bring a guarantor so that they would set me free and they would send a telegram to the battalion to verify my statement. I brought them a guarantor and they let me go.

The answer came back in a week saying that Megher and I were deserters. The officer told me to bring a guarantor again so that we could go home for two weeks before being sent to the battalion. I brought the same man as before when I was in the barracks in Aintab. God bless this man because he did so many good things for me. He helped me many, many times. I went home and then to the village with Misak and Melkon. After two weeks they went to my house to look for me and I was forced to go home and surrender. Misak and Melkon stayed in the village.

I went to the barracks and two weeks later, several families got permission to move to Aleppo. My son Mathios, with his mother, Melkon, and Misak with their families joined these people even though they did not have permission to move. They rented a cargo carriage with a Turk driver. I got to see them when they were passing by the barracks. I cried, and so did they. Mathios was a year-and-a-half old at that time. Then they left. When I was writing these words, my eyes got filled with tears and I stopped writing. That day I had to endure so much. I did not know where I was going or what I was going to do. Inside of me there was a fire, and I could not stop thinking about them. I offered money to the gendarmes so they would let me go, but they didn't.

After about a month, several hundred gendarmes were sent to the village and to the city. We came to a village and the first night we slept

---

* **Yarpuz is a village southwest of Kayseri.**
** **Kastamonu is a city in northern Turkey.**

at an inn. It so happened that Misak and Melkon, disguising themselves as Kurds, came to the same inn. They left in the morning before we saw each other. Misak's family met some people on the road with animals and became with friends with them. Our paths crossed again at the top of a mountain but we did not see each other. Later, while in Aleppo, we talked about this incident and realized that we had been so close to each other on the road. They said that they had seen the group of gendarmes but had not noticed me.

We arrived to Marash. I was the only Armenian in the thousand gendarmes at the barracks. Only two of them knew that I was an Armenian. One of them was from Marash, and the other Yarpuz. At that time, I was wearing clothing like a Kurd and had not shaved for about a year. One day, the commander of the barracks was looking at the names of the gendarmes and saw my name.

Wondering where I came from he called for me. He asked me where I had been for so long. I told him that I did not know what he was talking about. He said that it was written in the book that I was a deserter and asked me where my family was. I told him that they had gone to Aleppo when I was incarcerated. Then, he asked me if I would stay or escape if he kept me in the barracks. I told him that if he kept me there I promised I would stay, but if he sent me to another place I would escape at the first opportunity because I knew that my life would be in danger.

He did not listen to me and said that he was going to send me somewhere else and that if I could escape I should do it. He prayed for me, stood up, and left. At the time there were no Armenians in Marash. They had all gone to Aleppo. It is easy to tell the story, but you should think about how hard it was to go through it. I think death would have been easier than living a tormented and dangerous life. You will understand when you grow older. You couldn't possibly understand when you are young.

We were about a hundred gendarmes sent from Marash to the barracks. Again I was the only Armenian in this group. Twelve sergeants and two-hundred Turks from Aintab had come to the barracks to be dispatched from there. They would not come close to us outsiders, watching us like foxes. A Syrian Kurd was with us who had been caught in Aintab and sent to the barracks. I saw that he was talking with the sergeant. When they parted ways, I went to him and asked what he was talking about with the sergeant. He said that he was begging the sergeant to set him free, but the sergeant wanted money from him and he did not have any.

I told the Kurd to go ask him how much the sergeant wanted for the both of us and he said twenty-five coins. I agreed and told him to ask the sergeant when we could escape. The sergeant said that we could escape at five o'clock when his turn as guard was. He said that I should approach him to go out to use the bathroom, and as soon as I gave him the money he would let me go. Then, he would come by the Kurd and let him go too. We agreed.

The two Turk friends of mine had always told me not to escape alone because something could go wrong. They said that I could come to their village and spend time there when I escaped. All of my family had gone to Aleppo. All of the Armenians were there and having a hard time to survive. My two Turk friends asked me not to go there. Their advice didn't make sense to me, but they begged me not to go.

My eyes were filled with blood from crying too much every time I thought of my family. Anyway, it was four o'clock and I was eagerly anticipating my escape. The sergeant who we talked to came and was waiting for his turn as guard. Five minutes past five, I went to where the sergeant was and told him to let me go outside because I needed to use the bathroom. He took the gun from his chest and loaded it with a bullet. I started to worry, wondering to myself what was about to happen.

We went outside and he told me to give him the money. I gave him the money in the middle of the darkness. After we took fifteen steps forward, he told me to go by the tree and wait while he goes and brings the Kurd here. I told him to go first to get the Kurd, and then I'll turn around. He said, "No, you first," and I said, "No, you first." We went back-and-forth like that. This dog wanted me to give him my back so that he would shoot me and tell the others that I tried to escape. We argued for a few minutes like this.

Seeing that I was not going to budge, he told me to come close so that he would give the money back. He gave me the money back and we both went back for the Kurd. What happened to me that night I wouldn't wish on anyone. If I stayed I would be in danger, and if I left I was in danger. I thought that there was no way out. God helped me to come out safe.

When I went back inside the tent I saw my two Turk friends with pale faces. They thanked God a thousand times that they saw me alive. They told me that they were begging to God to protect me from danger thinking that any moment they would hear the shot. These two friends, even though they were Turks, were praying for my wellbeing. God bless them and give them long lives. This is the difference between the people of Elbistan and Marash. They are all Turks, but the ones from Elbistan were different than those of Marash.

We left in the morning. The other gendarmes had known that I was going to be killed the night before. One of them came close to my friends. After they talked, my friend told me that the gendarme told him that I had been wise like a wild pig because the guard could not shoot me last night. I did not talk to the Kurd again because he could have been in accordance with the guard to kill me.

We walked for a few hours. The gendarme was again talking to my friends and had told them that the 'nonbeliever' had three Osmanian liras. He told them that if they took the money from me and give it to him, he would let us escape. He would shoot to the sky pretending to come after me, but will stay where he was and let me go.

My friends told him that they would not harm me. God bless them again and give them long life because they saved me from this danger so that I could see the face of my son. That day we got to Osmaniye and they put is in an inn. We were like a thousand gendarmes and there wasn't a decent spot to sit. It was dirty everywhere and we had to accept it. It was prohibited to go outside to use the bathroom. A Turk with a can full of his urine came to me and said, "Nonbeliever, take this and throw it outside." I said that in all the people here he found me to do it? I said no. He went and brought a sergeant who forced me to do it.

I did not have a way out so I did as I was told.

We took the train in the morning from Osmaniye and arrived to Adana. At the time the French had already left. They accommodated us into a large and empty Armenian school. Between a thousand gendarmes I was the only Armenian. Nobody would notice if they did not call my name. When we were sleeping that night, a gendarme screamed, "Nonbeliever, where are you?" He called three or four times, but I did not answer.

One day, I went to the barber shop and saw that the barber was looking at me from the corner of his eye. I guess he was wondering what ethnicity I was. My attire was like the Kurds and he asked me where I was from and I answered that I was a Kurd from Elbistan. We stayed for several days in Adana until we left for the barracks by train. When the train stopped, more than two dozen people who were going to Ankara left the train, including me. They sent us to dispatch but my friends stayed in the train and went to Konya.

I was alone now. One night, more than a dozen people were talking about some bandits who got into Saimbeyli after it was surrounded by Turks for a year-and-a-half and the atrocities performed there. I sat there and listened to them about all the cruelties that had happened in Saimbeyli after the surrender of the city to the Turks. The stories they told me were saddening. Because of foreigners, bad things happened to Armenians. If I knew that I was going to survive I would have paid more attention to details to have everything documented by date.

Now that I am older in the year of 1958, I am writing again so that when you read this you will understand many things. I recommend that you do not lose this writing. Do not let the children tear or damage it. Keep it safe. Read it so that you will remember your parents and grandparents until you die, and learn from it and tell your children about it.

That day, they chose the names of the people who were going to Ankara. They called my name, so I approached and saluted. They told me to go to one side. When the other gendarmes heard my name, they were surprised and looked at each other saying that I wasn't Kurdish but Armenian.

They called about forty people and we continued toward Kayseri. After six days we arrived there. Again, they put us in an empty Armenian school.

It was close to Elbistan, but I did not have the opportunity to escape. When we went into Kayseri I realized that the sergeant who had pretended to take money from me to escape was there. He was always checking on me so that I would not escape. We stayed in Kayseri for four days and in the morning of the fifth day we left. We were about five-hundred people. We arrived at a police station near a bridge on the Kizilirmak. They had chosen the names of fifteen gendarmes who were going to Ankara, while the rest were going back to the barracks at the train station. Two sergeants took command and we started to walk. Nobody read our names because they were in a sealed envelope. That's why nobody knew who I was.

We stopped midway and ate some bread. We walked and reached the bridge on the Kizilirmak where the police station was. There was only one gendarme there and could not receive us. He said that there was another police station at Hacibektashli*. We started to walk again. When we arrived, they told us that there was a German shepherd in the police station that could bring a man down his horse, so they would tie it during the day and let it go free at night.

A year before, Misak and I had passed over this river from another bridge. Anyway, a young boy, who was the son of one of the commanders, was walking by our side. He used to talk to one of the sergeants. I asked him that he was talking to the sergeant too much and I wanted to know what they were talking about. He told me that there were two people who were offering the sergeant six coins to let them go.

The sergeant did not accept. I told the boy to go and ask the gendarme if he would let me go if I gave him sixteen instead of six, and that I would give the boy two coins as a tip. He went and came back telling me that the sergeant had accepted. I gave the money to the boy and the boy gave it to the sergeant. It was evening by now.

---

* Hacibektashli is a small village southeast of Ankara.

The sergeant came to me and told me to stay in the back of the group so that I could escape. I disagreed because the last gendarme could see me as I leave.

We were approaching a bridge, so I told him that I would hide under it while the group continued. When we got close to the bridge, I separated from the group and hid. They had walked for about ten minutes until they suddenly stopped. An officer had pointed out that one gendarme was missing and the sergeant tried to cover it up. Then, I saw somebody coming toward me. I thought that these people had taken my money and were going to stab me in the back.

Then I saw that the sergeant was approaching me, so I asked him what was wrong. He told me not to move and passed by. He came back and told me to wait for the darkness of night, then leave. I waited for them to go a little further away from me so that I could go to the other side in case they decided to come back for me. I decided to use that time to smoke two cigarettes.

Escaping On My Way to Adana

Night came. It was very dark. I got close to the bridge on the Kizilirmak and took my shoes off so that the German shepherd by the police station would not hear my steps or sense my presence. I then started to climb the mountain next to the police station. I walked for about an hour, but I kept looking around in paranoia and fear. It was scary being so close to the police station and the dog. I walked for two more hours until I reached a river. I walked for a while down the length of the river until I reached another bridge. I crossed the bridge and continued.

I did not know where I was going. I was walking in a large valley between mountains. After a few hours of walking, I heard the barking of a dog. I thought that I was close to a village. I started to climb the mountain some more, but did not know how high it went. I climbed for about an hour until I reached a plateau. All of the sudden I saw a bunch of partridges in front of me scattering. I sat there and smoked two cigarettes. Refreshed, I started to walk again.

I could have encountered any wild animal, but I never thought that I was going to see partridges. I climbed for another hour and got close to the top when the path started to go downhill. On this side of the mountain there were only small rocks and it was not easy to hold onto them while going down. I finally found the road to Kayseri and passed a few villages on my way.

I saw several travelers walking on the road, so I laid down to hide for a few minutes while they passed. I tried standing up again to move and realized that I couldn't. My legs weren't responding. I checked myself to see if I was wounded. I had been walking for twenty-eight hours straight. Even if I had legs of steel they couldn't carry me any further.

There was about an hour left to reach Kayseri, but in my mind I could not bring myself to continue. I saw a summer house nearby and went inside with the intention of eating something. I did not have any water and couldn't even swallow the bread I had. Hungry, thirsty, and tired, it was hard to endure.

I heard voices outside from people working in the fields. I did not want to fall sleep, so I would force my eyes open every time they closed.

I was afraid of sleeping because somebody could find me. I opened and closed my eyes like fifty times while sitting. I wanted to eat bread but could not, so I just sat there like that until midday. I had the idea of going to the field workers to ask for water. I went to go urinate when a boy who was picking up sticks saw me and went to go tell the others. I went by their side and said, "Salam alaikum." I asked them for some water, and after that they could ask me anything. One of them told the boy to go and get some water from the spring. After I drank I felt alive again.

It was Ramadan time, so they would not eat or drink at certain times of the day and they were working in the fields like that. We started to talk and I found out that they were also deserters, so I told them that I was a Kurd from Elbistan. One of them said that I could pass the villagers as a merchant, but I had no merchandise to disguise myself. It was afternoon and they went for ablution, to wash themselves and pray. I joined them thinking that maybe one of them would invite me to their home that night.

They took water from the spring and told me to wash my hand so that we could pray. I should have learned at the time how to pray like them. I asked them what kind of Islam they were, saying that I could not pray with dirty clothes and in my haggard state. If I prayed as I was, I would be committing a sin. They realized that I was not ignorant in the matter and I was able to skip the prayer.

It was night, every one of them carrying something on their shoulders. I was left alone again. I went back to the empty house in the fields and after resting for a bit I continued my journey. I got close to Kayseri and went in by one side. I did not find any Armenian to go to their house. Without any hope, I decided to go to an inn. I thought that I could rest for a few days. I encountered several children while I was walking and asked them where I could find a nearby inn and they answered that if I went straight that I would find one. I found the inn, went inside, and saw that several people were sitting there, one of them being a gendarme.

I asked the innkeeper if a carriage from Elbistan had passed through, and the said that they would not come to this inn but rather go to a different one. I asked him if there was anybody who I could give some money to so that they could take me there. He asked me why I had not traveled with them. I told him that my horse was ill and that I stayed with it until it died, which is why I did not know which inn they went to.

He called a boy and told him to take me to that inn. I saw that the boy looked Armenian, so I told him that I was also Armenian and asked him to take me to an Armenian's house. He took me to a neighborhood, and I saw women sitting outside in front of some of the houses but I did not have the courage to approach.

Then I asked him to take me to the church. At that moment, a young man came after us and asked us where we were going. The boy told him that he was taking me to the church. The young man told the boy to go home and that he would take me there. I tried to give some money to the boy as thanks, but he did not accept it.

We arrived to the church and discovered that the door was locked. I knocked on the door and the altar boy opened it. He asked us what was going on and I told him that I was an Armenian deserter and that I had nowhere else to go for the night. He told me to wait while he asked the priest. He came back and told me that the priest did not want me to stay. How could I keep my mouth shut?

I said that I had gone through so many difficulties. Hunger, thirst, sleeplessness, and on top of it all the priest didn't even want me in the church. I started to say all kinds of bad words. My ears did not want to hear the words that came out of my mouth. The young man did not hold back either, and said that if they had a little bit of mercy they would have accepted me. He ended up inviting me to his house.

They had become refugees for the second time during Mustafa Kemal's rule. They were very poor, a sister and a brother. The sister had recently married with an Armenian. When she saw me, she asked her brother why he had brought a Kurd to their home. The brother answered that I was an Armenian deserter, and she welcomed me and spread a piece of fabric on the floor so that I could sleep on it.

I used my bag as a pillow and slept. Then her husband came and asked who I was, and when he found out who I was, he also welcomed me.

In the morning, the men left. They came midday and we ate bread and onions, and at night we ate bread and yogurt. I stayed there for four days to rest. I told the young man that if he passed by the inns and saw a carriage from Elbistan to let me know. He would come every day and tell me that he had not seen it yet. From the fifty coins I had before, there was only five left. The fourth day I gave him one and told him to bring me bread and dried fruit because I was leaving.

I walked for a few hours. It was very dark, and suddenly I saw something that looked like a black bear ahead. I was paralyzed in fear. My feet would not move. If it was a bear, I had practically stepped into its jaws. I took out my knife so that if it got closer I would stick it into his belly.

I didn't notice any movement after a few minutes. If it was an animal it would have moved by now. The way it was standing looked exactly like a bear. I touched it and realized that it was a rock. A rock had scared me that much.

I sat on it and smoked a cigarette. I took a deep breath and continued walking. I passed by the same creek from the upper side of the police station where Misak and I had passed. This time, I went a little bit further up the creek. It seemed like the rocks were hit and broken by somebody, so it was very difficult to cross the water. I saw a hill in front of me, and on the other side of it there were small and sleek rocks which made it hard to walk or even crawl on them. It took me an hour to do what should have been only ten minutes. I lost my breath and sweat a lot. I sat and lit a cigarette, rested, and then continued my journey.

I walked for a few more minutes and found my path. It was almost morning at this point. I saw a small cave and went into it. I changed my clothes, put the bread on my chest, and wrapped my bag on my waist. I decided that I was not going to walk at night anymore. I had four coins, so if they caught me I would give them two coins and, hopefully, they would let me go.

I went into the road and reached a village by night. I went into the inn and ate something, then slept. In the morning, I started my journey again and joined some other travelers. Together, we walked for a while until they separated while I continued my path. After a few more hours, I encountered some other travelers. Three men and a woman. I greeted them, and together we went into the village.

Everyone went into their houses and I went after the woman. She went into a house, and I decided to go inside too. From the inside another woman asked who I was. The woman who had been walking with me answered that I was a traveler, but the other woman said that I was not welcome and told me to go to another house. She shooed me away like a dog. I went to another house, but they also rejected me. I thought to myself what a blessed day it was today. Either there were no Muslims in this village, or they did not accept traveler's anymore.

A man noticed me and asked me to approach him. He told me to come inside his house. He gave me a chair and brought me some food. After we ate, he said that he was going to go to his room to pray and asked me if I would join him. I told him that if I went with him I was going to dishonor God and him. He asked me why, and I told him it was because my clothes were dirty and that it would be a sin. He said okay and prayed alone.

After he prayed, his wife gave us some pajamas and we slept. When it became morning, I left. That day I went back to the road, far from the police station. I went to a village where the Afshar Tribe* lived. I told them that I was Armenian, and because they liked Armenians they let me spend the night there. I left in the morning. I was close to Elbistan.

It became night and I slept in Ercene**. There were only eight hours to go. I walked for five hours the next day. By midday I had reached the border of Elbistan, and I saw the sheriff who had caught me before. He was with some other people, and they were by the water to wash and pray. I recognized them all, but they did not recognize me. I sat there and saw them going into the mosque.

---

* The Afshar people are a nomadic people who primarily live in Turkey, Iran, and Azerbaijan.
** Ercene is a village just west of Elbistan.

I went to my uncle Yeprem's house. His wife and daughter were sitting there. One of their neighbors was Turkish, so I went straight inside to avoid him.

Yeprem's wife looked at me with incredulousness thinking that a Kurd stranger was randomly barging into her house. I told her to be quiet, and Yeprem's daughter recognized me voice saying that I was Avedik. We sat together for a while.

I then went to Mihran Magarian's house and ate there. They gave me clean clothes while I took a bath. I stayed for a few days and rested. It had been two-and-a-half months since I had seen my wife, so I wrote a letter to her telling her that I was healthy. When my wife received the letter, she thanked God for saving me from danger so that Mathios could see his father again. Saying it and writing it is easy, but going through it was hard. Praise God that he keeps you from these kinds of situations. Amen.

I left Mihran's house and went to a Turk friend's house, staying there for a few days. After, I stayed with some Kurd friends in the village. I spent almost two months there. Then, I went to another village and two Turks who I knew said to me that a few days from then, they would finish a job and go to the city to buy fabric to work with. I went with them into the city, and for three days we shopped for fabrics.

We came back to the village and worked with the fabrics, sold them, and went back to the city to do everything all over again. After we finished, I took my part of the profit and went back to the village. I had thirty kilos of olive oil. I put it on top of a mule and went on the road by night. In the morning I entered the city.

I saw that there was no one in the houses of the Armenians, so I became suspicious. I went to the house of a Turk whose wife was from Aintab, and told her that I could not see the Armenians from Aintab. I asked her if they had died. She told me that it had been eight days since they gathered all of the Armenians and stuffed them into a hotel without letting them leave. They were going to send them to Aleppo. The news broke my heart.

I asked the woman to get her son, and then I asked her son to get the father whose house I was staying in. The man came, and his name was Nalband Nemed. I asked him what was going on, and he said that they were going to deport the Armenians again. I gave him the olive oil that I had and told him to go and sell it, and to give me the money later. Three Armenian women came to that house to do laundry.

I asked them to go and give notice to Mihran and my relative Sarkis to come to me. When they came, I told them that I did not know what would come when they were all gone and that I did not want to be left alone. I asked them to talk to the lieutenant for a permit so that I could go with them to Aleppo. The lieutenant said yes because he was good with the Armenians.

They were going to leave in two days, which was not enough time for me to leave with them because I was still owed six Osmanian liras from several villages that I had to collect from before leaving. It would have taken me ten hours just to get to the first village, but I decided to go anyway. Fifteen minutes after leaving, two gendarmes came after me saying that the lieutenant wanted to see me.

I did not know why the lieutenant was after me. I later heard that the lieutenant had sent news to my Turkish friend to go and see him, and had asked about the olive oil that I had given him. He said that he had sold it and the lieutenant asked for the money, to which my friend answered that he couldn't.

Anyway, it was five o'clock when I arrived at a village. The landlord was sitting on the roof of the house. He welcomed me, then asked me if there was any good news. I told him that I had too much to do and that I had to do everything fast because they were deporting Armenians. He told his wife to go and bring me food. After I ate, I wanted to leave but he told me to stay there that night and did not let me go.

I arrived at the first village early in the morning and went to my friend Hassan's house. I asked him if he could come with me to collect some of the money. I told him I would give him any wheat that they offered me for a little bit of money. We went to four villages and gathered three Osmanian liras. I gave him my good clothes and told him that I was going to leave at night. We were very sad to separate, so we cried. I wished for God to give him whatever he wanted, and he asked God to help me and keep me alive.

I went to the road and in ten hours I was back in the city. I slept only three hours in three nights. I went to see my friend who I had given the olive oil to sell, and took the money that he had for me. He told me about the lieutenant, and I told him that he did a good job.

I went to the hotel by the Armenians. After three days, men came and started to put our belongings on the carriages.

The Marashian gendarmes used to make fun of them so that they would do everything faster and leave. Anyway, we left through the market and onto the road. A few gendarmes came with us to protect us. We had walked for about an hour, and a gendarme on horseback came after us and told us to stop. He said that the lieutenant had given the order for us to go back to the city, so we returned.

Now, we were wondering what they were going to do with us. We went back into the hotel. Some of us went to the lieutenant to ask him what was going on, and he told us not to be afraid. He said that he received news that the road that we were traveling on had bandits who were going to attack us. They thanked him and left. We were ten Armenian families.

We left in the morning to the village road, and this time ten gendarmes came with us for protection. The lieutenant saw me and approached me with his horse. He mentioned me by name, asking me where I had been for so long. I answered him that I had been here and there over to friends' houses, and he said that he had heard of me coming to town. He said that he didn't send gendarmes after me because he felt sorry for me. I thanked him and said, "God give you a long life."

That day, we went into a village which was populated by the Cherkess*. Even though it was dangerous to stay there, he sent guards to stay with us at night. The ten gendarmes that were with us were from Elbistan. The lieutenant had told them to take us alive and healthy to our destination saying that if someone came to him claiming they mistreated us, they would be in big trouble. I will never forget the humanitarian help that the lieutenant gave us. In every culture and ethnicity, there are the good and the bad.

*** The Cherkess, or Circassians, are a group of people from the North Caucasus near the border of present-day Russia.**

We arrived to Selamet* village and they put us in somewhere again. We stayed for eight days there while we sent a telegram to Aleppo telling them that us ten families had left Elbistan and were coming to Aleppo through the villages so that they knew that we were coming. We signed the telegram Aghbabian, Magarian, and Avedik. My brother and my wife were very happy when they knew that I was with the group. After ten days, we left with the other gendarmes.

We arrived close to a river and Arsen caught some fish there. At meal time, the gendarmes sitting with us started to say bad things about us, saying that the dog would not forget to eat dirty food and asked us if we had been deported in the past.

We said yes, but we didn't understand what they were trying to say. They asked us to give them money to spend and we said that if they took us alive and healthy to Marash, we would give them the money. They asked us again on the road several times, but we did not give them anything.

When we arrived to Marash, we did not give them any money. When we left Elbistan, we had given our money to a merchant so that when we arrived to Aleppo another merchant would give us the equivalent there. We found a carriage driver from Kilis** to take us to Aleppo. We arrived to Kilis and they took us to the border, but we did not know if we were on Turkish or Syrian land. We were afraid that we would get robbed. We walked for a half hour more and saw several militia who came by us on horseback, taking the Turkish carriage drivers with them. The drivers, crying and begging, were asking to be let free. A few of us went by them and brought the drivers back.

We then entered Azaz*** and stayed there for a night. We were in Aleppo the next day, alive and healthy. I went to my house. The year was 1924. I was lucky to have survived countless atrocities, and even luckier to be reunited with my loved ones.

Many, many other Armenians did not have the same fortune. Many

---

* Selamet is a village in northeastern Turkey near the coast.
** Kilis is a town in southern Turkey on the Turkey-Syria border just north of Aleppo.
*** Azaz is a town that lies in Syria just further south of Kilis.

were executed, starved, or worked to death. Even worse, these acts were placed upon us by the very people that we lived alongside. No one could have foreseen such a horrific thing to happen like that.

It is important to remember the Armenian Genocide, and other genocides, so that such things never happen again. We must hold onto truth.

Life after the Genocide

And so I came from Elbistan to Aleppo in 1924. I did not have any profession or money. I started to earn my living by fishing. Not having experience in any profession, I had to do what I could to get by. More or less, I could cover the household expenses on my own. One day in the summer, we had gone to the Murad River* to catch some fish with my brother Dikran. He had quit his job and had stayed with me for two weeks.

That day, I found another two people to help us. The previous two who were helping me had decided to quit. The four of us got on a raft made of wood and sheepskin tied together and inflated with air. We floated to the middle of the river to throw the net and catch some fish. We encountered a strong current, and reached a point where one side of the river was shallow and the other was deep. We moved to the shallow side and saw a rock in front of us that was about five or six meters high, and another rock on the other side that was four meters high. In between there was about a meter to pass.

The raft was going to hit the rocks, and we were going to lose both our lives and belongings. We could not maneuver the raft because of the strong current. I went into the water so that when the raft would reach the rock I could hold on. When I went into the water, it covered me until my ears. My feet were gliding over the slipper bottom of the river while the raft dragged me with it.

I had to leave the raft, and the moment I did so I was taken away by the current. The current took me about a hundred meters away, and when I opened my eyes, I realized that I was in the middle of a vortex. I didn't know how to swim.

Since I had been at the back of the raft, nobody realized that I had gone into the water. They had gone through the two rocks without an issue, and it was only after they realized that I wasn't with them that they started to look for me.

Wearing clothes and not knowing how to swim, I swirled with the vortex. I moved my hands and feet in any way I could trying to stay

---

* The Murad River lies southeast of Erzurum.

afloat. A woman started to throw rocks at me from the border of the river. I did not know what that woman was doing there.

It seemed like she thought I was just swimming. I shouted at her saying, "I am drowning here and you are throwing rocks at me?"

And on top of it all, since I had opened my mouth it got full of water. I got closer to a large rock by flailing as hard as I could, barely holding onto it with my nails and fingers. The water rose all of a sudden, so I held onto a higher part of the rock. When the water level dipped again, I stayed where I was. I thought that God had saved me and that somebody would come and help me.

One of my friends called me and told me not to be afraid. I answered that I was not afraid, but asked how he was going to come by my side. He came close and held out his hand. I extended my hand, and he pulled me up to safety. I went by the others, took out my clothes, and spread them so that they would dry.

My face was pale in fear. It seemed like a miracle had happened. At the end of the day, we went back to Aleppo. It was days like this that I was reminded of how fragile life can be.

In 1929, on Great Lent Monday, we were going to Tel Abiad. Five of us were in a small Ford car. We passed by Maskanah* toward Ain Issa. In the desert, there was a small canal that we came close to. About half an hour away from Ain Issa we saw a couple Arab men appear from the canal who sat in the middle of the road in front of us.

I knew that something bad was about to happen.

Prior to this, we had passed through the same road a hundred times without ever coming across people sitting in the middle of the road. We started laughing. The Muslim driver asked us if we wanted to go back. We asked him if he was local to Aleppo as a joke because he was afraid of every little thing.

Anyway, he continued driving. We were about a hundred meters from the two men when three more of them showed up with guns aimed at us. The driver to turn the car to go back. We heard four shots aimed in our direction, so we stopped and they approached.

---

* Maskanah is town in northern Syria.

We stepped out of the car while they looted anything that was inside. They were so hungry that you could see it in their eyes. We were carrying a lot of food: oranges, dates, seeds, onions, arak, and desserts.

We found out that that year there had been a hunger, so these people were desperate for food.

So they started to eat our food, and after they were full, they checked us for anything valuable. They took whatever they could find, including any money that we had. One of them got into the car and told the driver to drive away.

The rest of them took us to where they lived. They started to drink the arak, and they ate some more food as snacks. They were speaking Kurdish, Arabic, and Turkish. We suspect that they were from Turkey, so we got afraid. But they were Syrians from a local tribe. If we had known prior that they were local Syrians, we would not have been so afraid.

They checked us again to see if they had missed anything. I had two coins on me that they had not found the first time. The guy slapped me on the face asking me why I hid the money. They took our clothes, shoes, and even our socks. To top it off, they cursed us.

Some people joined in to come to our aid, both Arabs and Armenians. They told us to leave, but we asked how they expected us to leave without shoes. They told us that this was the desert and that we could go wherever. From where we were, Ain Issa was 30 kilometers away.

By this time it was dark and they left us alone. We learned that before robbing us, they had robbed two trucks. One had been a passenger truck, and the other a delivery truck. They hid the trucks in the canal.

At midnight, we reached Ain Issa. We went into someone's house and met some people. We kissed the hand of the head of the house. He told us to sit. They brought us food, and after we finished eating, he asked us what was wrong. We told him what had happened, and he asked if the robbers were Arabs or Kurds. We told him that they spoke both languages. He told us that he did not know them.

The next morning, he told his son Nuri to get five armed men and go to where the robbers lived. So Nuri went and found both the trucks and our car. The car was completely empty.

We later discovered that night on the night of our capture, one of the truck owners and our car driver drove the bandits close to the border of Syria and Turkey.

They reached a summit and the driver told them that they were already in Turkey, so the bandits left the car on foot thinking that they were safe.

The Tel Abiad governor was informed the next day about this incident. He deployed forty soldiers with military vehicles. Both Nuri and the soldiers went to three or four villages in search of the bandits. They found guns and detained fifty people. They took them to Tel Abiad and were put in jail.

That afternoon, Nuri did not come back to his house. His father was very worried. He ordered his men to get on horses and search for Nuri. While they were preparing to leave, one of them saw a car that approached. Nuri's father told his men to wait and see who was coming.

It turned out to be our car with a few men in it, one of them being the governor. He told us that Nuri was helping them to fight against the bandits. Since the car had run out of gas by the time it got back to us, we asked Nuni's father for some gas.

We drove to Tel Abiad in the next morning. We rested a bit on the road, and we got to Tel Abiad we reported our stolen things to the police. The police told us that they would search for the bandits and give us our belongings back.

The police took us to the prison so that we could identify any of the fifty people who had been caught prior. It was easy to tell that the prisoners were not guilty. We only reported three of them, so the others were released.

The released prisoners knew who the bandits were, but were afraid to give any information away because they were afraid for their lives. The three guilty men were sent to Deir ez-Zor. Two of them got two years later, while the third died in prison. Five years later, we met the two of them in Tel Abiad. They told us that they were afraid of telling the truth because they were scared of the bandits.

A year after that, I saw one of them wearing my fur. I would have asked for it back but I think that the man would have fought me for it.

Our black fate is like that. It is like we did not have enough darkness in our lives. How I endured all this time, I do not know. As I write this at the age of 70, I haven't even had 70 cents worth of happiness in all my life.

Even though I had survived the Armenian Genocide, I could have lost my life in a completely different way.

Life didn't stop after such a horrible time in history. I needed to sustain and provide for my family. I needed to move forward, despite the memories I had to carry with me.

Every day felt like life could slip away at any moment. Just like it is important to remember the Armenian Genocide, and remember our past, it is also just as important to not take the present moment for granted.

Live life to the fullest, because we don't know what the future holds. I was born with a burden and I will die with it. May the Lord not separate me from my faith. Amen.

www.ingramcontent.com/pod-product-compliance
Lightning Source LLC
Chambersburg PA
CBHW020621300426
44113CB00007B/731